## The Foreign Policy Centre

## www.fpc.org.uk

The Foreign Policy Centre is an independent think-tank committed to developing innovative thinking and effective solutions for our increasingly interdependent world. We aim to broaden perceptions of what foreign policy is, revitalise public debate about foreign policy goals and find new ways to get people involved. The Foreign Policy Centre publishes books and reports, organises high-profile conferences, public lectures and seminars, and runs major in-house research programmes on cross-cutting international issues.

For details of current and forthcoming publications, please see the back of this pamphlet. Individual publications should be ordered from:

GW00771586

Central Books
99 Wallis Road
London E9 5LN
T + 44 (0)20 8986 5488
F + 44 (0)20 8533 5821

For further information about the Centre, including subscriptions, please visit our website

or contact us at info@fpc.org.uk

## About the Author

Yasmin Alibhai-Brown is Senior Researcher at The Foreign Policy Centre. She has a weekly column in *The Independent*, and also writes for *The Guardian*, *The Observer* and many other newspapers, and broadcasts regularly on Radio 4 and the World Service. Her most recent book is *Who Do We Think We Are? Imagining the New Britain* (Allen Lane/The Penguin Press) and her previous books include *The Colour of Love, True Colours* and her autobiography *No Place Like Home*.

# After Multiculturalism

Yasmin Alibhai-Brown

**The Foreign Policy Centre**

First published in 2000 by
The Foreign Policy Centre
Panton House
25 Haymarket
London
SW1Y 4EN
T 020 7925 1800
F 020 7925 1811
E info@fpc.org.uk
www.fpc.org.uk

© The Foreign Policy Centre 2000

All rights reserved
ISBN 0-9535598-8-2

Printed in Great Britain by
Direct Image

Cover and Design by
Interbrand Newell and Sorrell

Typesetting by
Emphasis London

# After Multiculturalism

## Acknowledgements

Many of these ideas were first tried out on the readers of my column in *The Independent* and my book *Who Do We Think We Are?*, published by Penguin in the spring of 2000. I thank my readers who responded both positively and furiously to what I was saying. Their letters and emails forced me to reconsider and shape up the arguments. The reviews of my book revealed some interesting attitudes. White middle class men appeared to understand the spirit of what I was saying much better than those who believe themselves to be experts on race, particularly black academics who have grown comfortable within old multiculturalism. Both sets of responses stimulated new ideas. Thank you to Sunder Katwala, who spent hours making this come out right, and to Mark Leonard, whose critical support I value enormously. I want to thank the rest of the young and delightfully open team at The Foreign Policy Centre where no-one is ever too busy to help you out. I am grateful to Richard Stone of the Lord Ashdown Trust for providing financial support for this project. My hope is that the pamphlet will begin a long overdue national debate on a subject which has been circumscribed for too long.

London, May 2000

# Foreword by Mark Leonard

"What's multiculturalism got to do with it anyway?" is one of the answers given in Yasmin Alibhai-Brown's survey of young Londoners. And the question could well be put to a foreign policy think-tank publishing in this area. As Yasmin points out, the debates about multiculturalism and foreign policy in this country have often been strangers to each other in a way that has limited and constrained both. Linking them up, as The Foreign Policy Centre is trying to do, is vital because when we define and describe our national identity – and our attitude to diversity – we are also defining what role we will play in the world

If British identity is defined primarily through a desire to preserve our political and cultural institutions in their current form, a pride in our heavy industrial heritage, and an adherence to Protestantism, our foreign policy will be driven by a defence of national sovereignty, a mistrust of multilateral institutions and a fear of immigration on cultural grounds. If, on the other hand, we define Britishness according to values rather than institutions or religion, and celebrate Britain's global links, its openness to other cultures, its democracy and its creativity, then we will have a foreign policy based on pooling sovereignty with others to solve shared problems, building effective forms of international engagement and immigration policies suited to our economic needs.

This shows that we will not be able to agree on many international policy areas – from joining the Euro to sending troops to Kosovo – until we have resolved many questions about Britain. That is why Yasmin's argument that discussions about diversity cannot be left to members of so-called 'ethnic minorities' is so important. One of the most exciting achievements of this Government has been to take the debate about Britishness seriously and to begin to sketch out what a modern, forward-looking identity could look like. The challenge now is to link the different strands of the domestic debate to create a sense of what our role in the world should be.

But the debate about Britishness and multiculturalism has

wider consequences still. Identity is set to be perhaps the defining issue of the new millennium – and it is the task of progressive forces to show that we can shape this debate to strengthen
our emerging international community, rather than getting
caught in a much vaunted 'Clash of Civilisations'. Progressive
politics must be about harnessing the opportunities of the revolution in global communications, the spread of democracy and
economic interdependence – but we also need to understand that
the way in which settled ideas of political community are being
challenged can be threatening. Unless we manage to define
national identity so that it draws on our outward-looking history
and celebrates diversity, it will lead some to seek to retreat in
older, safer and more exclusive forms of identity defined along
ethnic, or religious boundaries. The task is to develop new forms
of internationalism that mesh with and complement strong
inclusive national identities – if not nationalism will become a
force which is pitted against globalisation.

Identity has been a major theme for much of the Centre's early
work. Questions of what Britain stands for, and the relationship
between policy-makers and public have dominated work on
everything from the European Union and the Commonwealth to
modernising diplomacy and defining the rights and responsibilities of NGOs in global governance. We have been considering a
specific contribution to the British debate about multiculturalism for some time. The turning-point came during last season's
party conference season. We were involved, with the
Commonwealth Institute, in holding two fringe meetings on the
subject of 'Delivering Multiculturalism', designed to address the
post-Lawrence report debate in a way which did make the links
between the domestic and the global. At the Labour Party
Conference in Bournemouth, Yasmin shared a platform with
Paul Boateng, Trevor Phillips and myself to discuss these issues.
We debated the same theme at the Conservative conference a
week later, with Anne Widdecombe and Matthew d'Ancona.
Those two debates were probably the most exciting and involved
which I have seen at any Party Conference. At both conferences,
we discovered a sense of frustration with the terms of the debate,
which were increasingly failing to connect – either to the people

in the audience (who were overwhelmingly black and Asian), or to the 'white majority', or to areas of policy which were not covered by the Home Office. This pamphlet is an attempt to open up a debate about what diversity means to all areas of policy – and to bring all sections of the population into a debate whose conclusions must be of collective interest.

It is with great pride that we publish Yasmin Alibhai-Brown for the first time. She joined the Centre at the end of last year – and has brought with her a wealth of experience of international issues as well as a deep sense of the links between the foreign and domestic debates. She continues to publish prolifically which is testimony not just to the quality of her work, and the strength of her voice, but also to the fact that she is able to engage with and write about an extraordinarily diverse range of subjects with power, passion and insight. I can't say that I agree with absolutely everything that Yasmin writes – but then probably nobody does. Her independent spirit is probably her greatest quality. She has never been afraid to examine and take on the unreflective shibboleths of those who might have thought that she would be 'on their side' – whether they come from Asian communities or the liberal chattering classes. This rare quality of Yasmin's work explains why – since she joined the Centre but somewhat coincidentally – she has been laden with awards from the CRE's special award for services to journalism to the Achievement in Writing awards at this year's Network East Live Mega Mela, as well as being highly commended in this year's Orwell Prize. And, if Yasmin brings a fairly unique perspective to the broadsheet press in this country, that is surely just as true of this contribution to the debate about how we understand foreign policy and international relations.

*Mark Leonard is Director of The Foreign Policy Centre*

London, May 2000.

# 1. Introduction: What's wrong with multiculturalism?

*She's 21, her mother is French; her father is from south India. She lives in Camden and studies law. Her sister's new-born baby is half-Senegalese. You might think of Tamsin as the living embodiment of our multicultural society. But she doesn't want to bear that role: "I don't want other people to tell me who I am. My friends don't give a damn about my cultural background. They like individual, free-thinking me".*

And Tamsin is not alone. There are many deeper anxieties stirring – and multiculturalism doesn't seem able to answer them. There are increasing numbers of people for whom multiculturalism simply doesn't connect any more.

This includes many of us for whom selling multiculturalism has been a life-long project, vocation and at times a burden. We have made progress. But, twenty-eight years after arriving in this country, I am still frequently asked, 'where are you from?' For all the talk of multiculturalism, people who look like me are not ever expected to be of this country. The questioner cannot accept Ealing or London. Only elsewhere will do. And so the oft-repeated explanations follow. I am *originally* from Uganda, from where we Asians were expelled by the military dictator Idi Amin. He did this to gain populist support and to further his political ambitions. Asians were much resented at the time because of their wealth and their failure to shed old prejudices about the inferiority of

Africans. The situation in Zimbabwe today is not dissimilar. I arrived in London in 1972 when the country was in the grip of Powellism. We will never return to those days, and much has changed and improved. But few would argue that we have the optimistic and integrated society which we would wish for. In fact there is evidence of greater separation into smaller tribes than ever before. Three decades of multicultural discourse, policies and strategies have achieved only superficial change. I believe it is time to kill off our old British multiculturalism and move on.

And it is vital that we do this now – when we have an opportunity to replace multiculturalism with something better. Muddling on is not an option. Questions of culture and identity are more central to British politics than they have been for two centuries. It is quite a shock for a country which thought of itself as old, settled and stable to find itself grappling with so much change at all levels and at unprecedented speed. Devolution, Europe and the Euro, the 'new economy', the internet and globalisation all raise central issues about identity – and tempt many to retreat to older and safer places. A nation which has prided itself on an unreflective pragmatism finds the bookshops and review pages are full of *The Death of Britain, The Day Britain Died, After Britain* and *Who Do We Think We Are?* There is a widespread sense that we do not really know any more and a related fear that devolution has set into motion a process of fragmentation and re-invented nationalisms which will imperil the ideal of an open state with diversity at the heart of it. A MORI survey for *The Economist* revealed that only 18% of Scots and 27% of the Welsh identified with Britain. In England, the figure rose to 43% but even here 41% described themselves as English and 49% felt an affinity with their regions above all else. Only 22% of all those interviewed felt confidence in our national parliament at Westminster.[1] These issues may turn out to be a key dividing line for politics in the next election. Developments in

Scotland, the increasing demands for an English parliament and the emerging group of influential conservative commentators are creating pressures which cannot be ignored by those on the centre-left.

But if the next great debate is between forces of internationalism and isolation, we will find that multiculturalism is perhaps surprisingly ill-equipped to promote internationalism – for it has often been as insular as its opponents. The debates which we have started to have about identity demonstrate how, for all of the battles fought over it in the past and the celebrations of multiculturalism today, we have not managed to *collectively* set up a national conversation in which we can talk through together what it means for a ethnically and culturally diverse society to be socially cohesive, equitable and successful. This will be difficult at times. It may involve questioning long-held and comfortable assumptions for all involved. But we can not avoid or duck it any longer.

There is an urgent need to engage in a collective project to define who we are as a people in this new century – so that we can share an outward-looking internationalism. But this means escaping from the restrictions that multiculturalism and the way we think about it have imposed on the stories that we can tell about ourselves. We need to reimagine our collective culture with ties that bind, when the old multiculturalism debate is still looking inwards, erecting new barriers between groups in our own society, instead of enabling us to collectively benefit from our diversity.

## The trouble with multiculturalism

The multiculturalism debate no longer connects. It doesn't offer a shared narrative of who we are today and what we stand for: it doesn't speak to young people or capture their identities, aspirations and the way they feel about the world. When the key issues transforming identities and opportunities include Europe, globalisation, the internet and cultural crossover, interactions and fusion, it too often has little or nothing to say about these. Multiculturalism is a simpler, narrower concept built around the assumptions of the past – and one which now holds us back.

## Multiculturalism is only about the 'ethnic minorities'

Multiculturalism has been seen as something that black folk do, entirely located in domestic urban politics and policies. These assumptions have shaped the entire discourse on multiculturalism in this country, as it has been developed both by white and black Britons. It has kept multiculturalism in a box – of interest to 'ethnic minorities', meaning those with visibly different skins. Because there are only 5-6% of us nationwide – somewhere between 3 and 4 million people – multiculturalism is therefore a marginal rather than national question. It may be of particular concern to a few of our larger cities, especially parts of London such as Newham, where these minorities make up 40-60% of the population. But just because there are places which are, by definition, multicultural, this need not have any effect on great swathes of the country.

## Multiculturalism has created a sense of white exclusion

There is, at one level, a broader consensus than ever before about how this country has irretrievably changed. Ethnic mixing is a central feature of urban life and is irreversible. And almost all public figures, from the royal family to the businessmen and the bishops, politicians of both left and right, the editors of red-top tabloids as well as liberal broadsheets, will now celebrate, from food to fashion, films to football, the new opportunities which diversity brings. But this does not itself tackle the problems of exclusion, of racism, or of the assertion of rights which conflict with each other. And, while multiculturalism may be embraced by a good many Britons, it is also resented by many others – who feel that everybody's culture is celebrated but their own, and that special treatment and disproportionate attention is being given to small minorities, whether black, Asian, Scottish or Welsh. And the multiculturalism debate has not recognised the many ways in which the various political and cultural anxieties of whites and non-whites alike are similar and inextricably linked. The irony is that, just as many black, Asian and progressive white Britons were just beginning to feel that the idea of Britishness was being broadened in a way that could also include them, we may be left rallying around the reclaimed flag only to find that there is nobody else there – leaving us as some of the newest and yet also the last Britons left.

## Multiculturalism's model of representation only deals with elites

And the glitzy, talked-up version of multiculturalism probably means even less, for example, to many British Pakistanis and British Bangladeshis, officially among the poorest groups in Britain today. 80% of British Pakistanis have incomes which are below half the national average. As one unemployed young black man interviewed for this report put it: "Celebrate what? This life? All that talk is for guys like Trevor Phillips and Paul Boateng with their expensive suits and white ways". Many of the black and Asian individuals who have reached the top of their careers in the arts, sport, the professions, the media or politics have inspired people through their achievements – and have often responded to their 'role model' status by helping many others too. These achievements are increasingly recognised in our institutions. More successful black and Asian businessmen and cultural figures have been made peers of the realm than ever before. But how far can they be expected to represent 'their communities' in the public sphere? The approach of counting heads by ethnicity goes throughout society and is often a easy way to avoid looking much more deeply at what the institutions actually do.

## Multiculturalism freezes change and can entrench inequalities

Multiculturalism was invented as a progressive project to promote and to equalise opportunities. But today it can too often do the opposite. In fact, traditional multiculturalism has allowed an alliance of convenience between the powerful. Post-war British political elites thought that civic peace required 'immigrant communities' to be kept separate: they could carry on with their religious and cultural practices as long as they did not make too many demands on the state and its majority culture. Traditional members of the 'immigrant' communities have found this most satisfying as it has kept their own power within families and communities intact, giving them influence as the cultural intermediaries between those who hold power and the 'ethnic' communities.

There has been too little interrogation of assumptions about transplanted cultures, or questioning of who is constructing these particular versions of their traditions and why. In practice, this has meant at times tolerating, overlooking or legitimising human rights abuses. In the black and Asian communities men and women share the experience of suffering racism but have yet to sort out the repressive sexism which blights their communities. Racism is, in fact, used as an excuse not to deal with sexism by far too many black and Asian people. So whose multiculturalism is it anyway? And multiculturalism often fails to understand how immigration transformed both those who came to stay and those who were already here, and how the world is in the process of unstoppable change.

## Multiculturalism erects barriers, when it ought to unite

But a distorted form of multiculturalism has increasingly become a banner under which increasingly differentiated groups each pursue their own case for attention and resources, while jealously protecting their rights not to be criticised by others. But this idea of our society as simply a non-interference pact between different groups is not just wrong, it is impossible. We are all now necessarily involved with each other. There may be societies coming out of conflict where what academics call a 'consociational' approach – formally sharing power between groups – is perhaps the only way to create peaceful co-existence. But mainland Britain is not somehow a less pressurised version of Kosovo or Northern Ireland, with ethnic or cultural conflict simmering under the surface, a tinderbox of tensions liable to explode at any time, where different groups need to be placated. We can and must fully debate and resolve conflicts between equality, cultural rights and individual freedoms together.

## Multiculturalism is seen as woolly liberalism, not the competitive advantages of diversity

And we must do so from an understanding of the shared benefits which our diversity can and must deliver. Multiculturalism has always felt like such hard work to many, because it has for too long been presented as something that we ought to want. We need to realise that diversity is something that we can not afford to be without – and from which we can collectively benefit.

## Our island multiculturalism has not engaged with globalisation

For far too long multiculturalism has remained dislocated from Britain's foreign policies. The increasingly contested issues of Britain's role in Europe and the world – of this country's international objectives and identity – have bizarrely been almost entirely disconnected from the domestic debate about multiculturalism.

Post-war multiculturalism has, in fact, often been as insular and myopic, as the forces which have opposed it. So many countries are dealing with the challenges of making ethnically plural societies cohesive and successful, and yet multiculturalists very rarely talk to each other about the lessons which can be learnt. Canada, the Netherlands and the City of Berlin are all developing new and modern ways of redefining themselves in a cosmopolitan and diverse world. Rather than dealing with the complexity of their societies as a burden and threat to their old world, the political leadership in all three places has taken a positive and strategic approach. The traditional tendency of the British to believe that we are simply an example for all to learn from and have nothing to gain from the experiences of others has been as much a feature of the multiculturalism debate as of the British reluctance to engage with Europe. It is true that there is less overt and deep-seated racism in London than in Marseilles or Rostock but claiming that our race relations are incomparably superior to those almost anywhere else is too often an excuse for complacency and inaction. It helps to explain why multiculturalism has failed to shift or even really debate a national mindset that flows into a Palmerstonian fury whenever a Briton is involved in any incident *abroad*. A babysitter is arrested – in Massachusetts, USA, never mind Asia or Africa – and we immediately want to know why the justice system isn't up to scratch – 'who are these savages anyway?'

What, for example, has traditional multiculturalism done for attitudes to the European Union? Very little. Except for the widespread view among black and Asian people that Europe is a white fortress against the developing world or that we here in Britain are in some ways better off than those 'ethnic minorities' living in our partner countries, there is no engagement with the EU project. There is little understanding among fervent multiculturalists of how, for those who oppose diversity, the rejection of all things foreign comes as a package. Margaret Thatcher and Enoch Powell, who so feared 'their' country being swamped by black and Asian 'cultures', were also Europhobes. Stuart Hall says that "One of the problems with multiculturalism is that ethnic minorities only have a view about some issues which they think affect them directly. But they don't care about Europe. How can they not care about Europe?"[2] An estimated 16 million Muslims live in Europe. It seems they are in Europe but somehow not of it. Europe does not understand that Islam and Christianity have both been an intrinsic part of the west and far too many Muslims insist that they are apart from the west.[3] And so Europe and the multiculturalists have not connected, even on the 'my enemy's enemy is my friend' principle. And the European Union's projects and programmes are amongst the most old-fashioned, outdated and least likely to connect to real people's lives on offer anywhere. The Migrant's Forum, an unofficial body with no power and little influence, has no credibility among non-white Europeans because they still sing that old song about our marginality.

Multiculturalism, built around the images of 1950s Britain and 1950s immigrants, shows no real understanding of the complexity of our links with the rest of the world – the support from British Muslims for Bosnians and Kosovars; the flows of money from, say, British Bangladeshis which are almost never mentioned when looking at the government aid and official charitable donations which they quite probably dwarf; the Japanese businessman who is much part of this landscape as is the newly arrived Kosovar Albanian; the fact that there are almost as many Americans in Britain as people of Jamaican origin. Non-resident Indian (known as NRIs) are beginning to exert their influence in the United States, and in this country too, as star players in the global markets – they see the west as their base but are committed to ensuring that India is both enabled to share in the economic prosperity created by globalisation and preserves its cultural strengths. The Hindus who built the exquisite marble temple in Neasden raised the money through strong connections across the globe. When these links don't fit the neat multicultural story then they are left out and forgotten. The complexity of our real internationalism, our sense of the possibilities when identities move beyond the home and the hearth, is diminished.

## Why this matters

So old-fashioned multiculturalism is simply not strong, flexible or exciting enough to meet the needs of the 21st century. Some would argue that the term can be relaunched, resucitated and reinvented yet again – but I no longer think that one more heave can get us where we need to go. The multicultural mindset and ideology has reached the end of its useful life – it is the moment to dispense with these ideas and ways of thinking. In many ways the multiculturalism debate has enabled people to side-step the real issues of what happens, and what needs to happen, when a largely settled and racially homogeneous population is challenged by the entry of new people, with different world-views, different expectations and different myths too. I do not agree at all with the demonisation of multiculturalism by the right which still wants to cling to the illusion that the country can go back to the fifties and 'manage' the different communities by absorbing them. The liberal left has often moved the debate forward in ways that were neither 'woolly' nor ineffectual. But there can be little doubt that even laid-back liberals were enormously challenged when the Salman Rushdie affair erupted and the usual tools of benign tolerance were rendered useless.

**This isn't about a word – but about a way of thinking about people** and about the real choices we all make as a result. Identity – how we understand who we are and what we want to achieve – helps to determine what we do. Lives are affected. And so concepts do matter when they lead to different choices being made, to resources being allocated in a particular way, to different assumptions being favoured and promoted, to people being dealt with differently. As Professor Bhikhu Parekh of Hull University says: "Our inherited ethnic vocabulary is increasingly out of touch with reality and we need a new one. Britain today is not so much a multicultural society as a culturally heterogeneous society with cultural differences proliferating and spilling over into and subverting inherited ethnic categories".[4] We are at a cross-roads today – and so we need to find new ways of describing ourselves which don't box us in, and to ensure that multiculturalism doesn't lead us to make the wrong choices about our society.

**Nor is this a rejection of the history that we have lived through** and the battles which many of us have fought, and sometimes won. But it is a recognition that it is now time to move on. The multiculturalism debate has so often simply been about the right of minority groups to be or stay here – or to have their particular voices acknowledged in the public sphere. This next phase must be about collectively reimagining ourselves and the society in which we live. This can only be successful if everybody is engaged in it.

We will see that the multiculturalism debate both misrepresents our history, and keeps us stuck in it. It is an inadequate ideology for the 21st century. While progress has been made, it has been in limited and circumscribed ways. And it is indisputable that the multiculturalist policies which have developed over time have failed to satisfy most of the people – of all backgrounds – most of the time. Multiculturalism is getting in the way of our doing what we need to together – because it speaks not to our shared future, but much more to our past.

# Part One

# Multiculturalisms past and present

14   After Multiculturalism

# 2. How we got here: a brief history of multicultural times

Whatever the failings of the way the issue has been handled, genuine and irreversible change has taken place in this country since the Second World War: the country is more varied and complex than it ever imagined. But, while multiculturalism has evolved, it is still too constrained within the bounderies which we, black and white Britons, have constructed – and within an invented and partial history.

For three hundred years, Britain has been a global nation – in many ways, for bad and good, and it is this complex and interconnected past which shapes us all which is now being rediscovered. Shakespeare was a globally-inspired writer who brought us Italian families, Moorish lovers and strange islands. Look at eighteenth century paintings and it is astonishing how many black people feature. Mary Seacole, a black nurse, worked hand in hand with Florence Nightingale, and was much revered in this country. Maya Jaggi and Caryl Phillips have written often and well about the many diverse writers who have helped to shape British literature and identity over the years. They include other Europeans, Americans, colonial subjects, ex-slaves, the Irish, and English people born in the old colonies – Thackeray, Conrad, Kipling, Orwell, Jean Rhys, TS Eliot, Doris Lessing, CLR James, VS Naipaul, Ben Okri, Wilde, Yeats: "To exclude people from your present and future", warns Jaggi, "you must also partition and ethnically cleanse the past, purging 'outside' influences from memory". David Dabydeen has revealed the presence of 'blackness' in British art through the centuries. Peter Fryer and Rosina Visram have written essential texts on the long intertwined roots between black, white and Asian Britons.[5]

But for fifty years we forgot about these connections. The foundations of the multiculturalism debate were already therefore flawed, creating the boxes within which thinking, debate and policies about multiculturalism have been largely confined. While many of the leading thinkers about multiculturalism have sought to shift and re-examine these boundaries, the debate is still confined by the core narratives, assumptions and myths of the second half of the 20th century – where the challenge was of immigration, understood as a new and unprecedented encounter, requiring the assimilation of 'alien' peoples and cultures into a 'host' society that now saw itself as homogenous and settled, which was of course liberal and tolerant but where the periodic threat of a particular 'influx' – whether Afro-Caribbean, Ugandan Asian or Hong Kong Chinese – threatened to upset the precarious balance. Difference was associated only with 'coloured' immigration, when as George Orwell says so lucidly in *England, Your England*, diversity is what defined and distinguished England, then synonymous with Britain.

Because of the myth that this country was, before the post-war immigration, a country entirely at peace with itself and settled in terms of its identity, the multiculturalism debate began from the premise that something needed to be done because these people with different cultures were arriving in such numbers. In fact, the Caribbeans were more British than the British. As Ros Howell, now in the Lords, says: "England was the only place to come ... it's like going to finishing school ... We didn't see England as a separate entity".[6] But, before the people who came off the Windrush had had time to have a bath, official panic about these people upsetting the national character was in full flight. Objections and anxieties were expressed by Labour and Tory politicians. Just as in previous times, when there was a concerted effort to ensure the gentrification of the great unwashed so that working class people could be brought into the fold of middle class civilization, black and Asian immigrants were processed so they could become trainee whites. As Ali Rattansi writes: "The assimilationist thrust was ... essentialist. Like all essentialism it assumes an obvious, definable, homogeneous essence (British culture) into which the hapless immigrant might be inducted".[7]

Roy Jenkins signalled a change in approach when, in 1966 as Home Secretary, he declared that the ideology of assimilation should be replaced with equal opportunity accompanied by cultural diversity. Jenkins was unique in his imaginative vision and this was a period of remarkable liberal consensus when leaders appeared to be breaking out of the old prisons where diversity was a threat. This was the first attempt from within the political establishment to recognise that difference could be positive – it is echoed in some of the most recent inspired developments in The British Council and the Arts Council. In the 'seventies and 'eighties, schools and other institutions attempted to translate this theology into practice by encouraging 'ethnic minorities' to feel pride in their own cultures and histories. This became known as the 'sari, somosa and steelband' version of multiculturalism – and it avoided the issues of racism or the low status occupied by those who wore saris, ate somosas and played in the steelbands. In the late 'seventies and 'eighties a more assertive form of multiculturalism began to be developed. This period of municipal anti-racism, most strongly associated with the Greater London Council and the Inner London Education Authority, took on the challenges of inequality and discrimination and used these to frame the arguments for multiculturalism. What was the point of Diwali celebrations in schools if the state neglected to provide older Asian Britons with interpreters when they went to the court or to hospital? And what difference did steelbands make to those who faced racial abuse and violence? People could not feel pride in who they were if they were constantly reminded that they were second-class citizens.

But, although it seemed possible to many involved at the time, a workable, exciting multiculturalism was not really constructed – still less maintained. Some local authorities understood the complex nature of this process but a few of them so misunderstood and mismanaged the process that it became easy for the entire project to be trashed. There was a right-wing backlash – a concerted and effective campaign from the tabloid press, the Tory government to the new right intellectuals writing in the Salisbury Review – which saw off this more potent form of multiculturalism. Remember Margaret Thatcher's fears that the country would be 'swamped' by alien cultures and her view that Europeans needed to take pride in the way they 'civilised' the rest of the world. But it is also important to recognise that even the most dynamic models of multiculturalism suffered from the deficiencies described earlier in this pamphlet. They were narrow, of minority interest, cut off from the concerns of the state at the time and the way society was being transformed. For example, as the concept of 'jobs for life' in traditional industries began to disappear, most multiculturalists failed to take that on board when arguing their case for equal treatment. For many white workers, terrified about the vulnerability of this new economic environment, trainers coming in and talking about multiculturalism made little sense. Some authorities took a punishing approach and alienated the most benevolent white people who were all made to feel culpable. Black and Asian people who were brought in through the multicultural doors were treated as undeserving and patronised at best, resented at worst. We need to understand why multiculturalism was powerless – in that it couldn't mobilise against the backlash. In any case, the battles of twenty years ago aren't going to deliver the solutions which our fast-changing society needs today.

Yet British multiculturalism remains trapped in its history. Perhaps even more than the setbacks and scenes of the mid-eighties, its disorientation was completed as the Rushdie affair produced new faultlines. Even Roy Jenkins was unnerved when the crisis arose and wrote about his misgivings about multiculturalism of this more demanding sort. Soon after *The Satanic Verses* was published Muslims in India started expressing their outrage saying that their prophet was being demeaned. The protests soon spread to this country – with calls for changes to be made or for the book to be taken off the shelves. These requests were ignored until one demonstration when the book was burnt in public. The liberal heart of this country was both shocked and repulsed. This evoked the images of Nazism – although the actions of the angry powerless can not be equated to the censorship of the absolutely powerful. Then came the fatwa which was passed by the Ayatollah Khomeni and had nothing to do with British Muslims. Rushdie's life was turned upside down and he spent the next decade living a hounded life. Liberal white people saw all Muslims as supporters of the fatwa, which most were not, and failed to understand the importance of the sacred to those with faith. Muslims failed to understand the values which liberals hold precious. The debate became polarised at fever pitch with no genuine dialogue or debate. If there were only two sides of this blazing conflict, then where did people like me fit in? We were at the same time alienated from the liberalism which had been the rock of our education and from Islam, because of the insane way in which it was manifesting itself.

But this showed how multiculturalism is much more challenging than previously imagined even by the fairest of us all. The murder of Stephen Lawrence produced the most recent national debate about race in Britain and revealed how thin and fragile multiculturalism is in Britain. The killing itself and the revelations of police failures so shocked the public that they brought the issues of racial violence into mainstream debate for the first time in two decades. The Lawrence family had to fight a long and determined campaign to get their voices heard. And the newly-elected Labour government acted bravely in creating the inquiry. But the sense of national unity and outrage may be fading. The media debate which followed the Macpherson report and which continues to rumble on, with a concerted effort to discredit his findings, emphasised how far the debate can remain entrenched in the battle-lines of the 1980s.

While the subject of multiculturalism has generated an enormous number of books, papers and conferences and inspired some of our greatest thinkers – Bhikhu Parekh, Stuart Hall, Homi Bhabha and Paul Gilroy – this has largely been a confab between friends. There has been much less infiltration of the best of these ideas into public policy. Most damagingly of all, there has been no concerted or effective strategy developed to dialogue with ordinary informed citizens, of the sort that Charter 88 managed so brilliantly on something that can seem as abstract and arcane as constitutional reform. There is no doubt that battles against racism will and must continue. They will require greater commitment, and for more people to feel positive about diversity. But it seems that multiculturalism is not delivering this. In fact, in society as a whole, it is losing its ability to connect.

# 3. "What's multiculturalism got to do with it anyway?" – how young metropolitan Londoners see themselves and their world

If multiculturalism is to have a future, it will be because people still feel that it can speak to their identities and aspirations, their values and what they want their world to be about. And it will be young people, in particular, who decide whether multiculturalism does this. Yet many seem to find that multiculturalism, because of the ways in which it is commonly understood and the assumptions which go with it, is irrelevant to them and their lives.

People's attitudes to diversity and identity are very complex and often confused. And so it is difficult to get much purchase on these from quantitative research. Poll questions on whether people regard Britain today as a multicultural society, or approve of this, produce percentage figures which are difficult to interpret without a broader picture of what lies behind these responses. The quantitative studies that occasionally take place are useful in order to track changing responses over time. But to get behind the numbers is more important. Even fairly racist people can self-censor themselves and know what the right thing to say is in quantitative studies, and the greatest challenge is to understand the complex views of those who think of themselves as tolerant, polite and non-racist. And these studies can do very little to examine or explain what people really mean when they say they are in favour of multiculturalism as a yes/no question. While there are now endless statistics on discrimination and how they affect black and Asian people, there are considerably fewer studies of what Britons collectively think about politics, society, race, identity and how we all fit together. Qualitative research is extensively used in Canada and the Netherlands but, despite claims that we live in a 'focus group culture', we in Britain rarely use what could be a very helpful tool for understanding attitudes to identity, race and society.

That is why I have found it useful to undertake both structured qualitative group studies and much more informal investigations. I have spent a great deal of time travelling and speaking to many people, far outside the usual circles in which I work, about these issues in all of their complexity. For this study, I was particularly interested in the views of multiculturalism amongst the young, and so I conducted further in-depth conversations with young people in London, which both the supporters and critics of multiculturalism would agree has been where the multicultural soul resides. These people could be seen to form multiculturalism's heartlands, its natural constituency, its 'core vote' as it were. These are the people that multiculturalism was designed to help. They have grown up with what we have thought of as multiculturalism – in their schools, through the media and in their friendships. And they seem to be outgrowing it in many and diverse ways – challenging its assumptions from different perspectives and identifying its blindspots, defining their own identities in ways which do not fit into the old multicultural boxes. Most are confident about themselves, their identities and their futures and many of them are natural internationalists. But they did not feel that multiculturalism adequately described the ways they interact themselves, that it would be important to them in creating opportunities for them to achieve their goals, or that it defined the type of society that they wish to live in.

## New survey data with young metropolitan Londoners

Thirty young people were interviewed to simply test whether they thought the concept of multiculturalism meant anything to them. Participants came from four racial groupings – white, black and Asian (including Chinese) and mixed-race. Initial interviews were carried out in same race groups of four followed by second interviews in mixed groups of four. They were aged between 15 and 24, and all of them were in full time education.[8] Although guided, these qualitative interviews were not structured around specific questions, but were designed to explore the following four areas:

- What does multiculturalism mean to them? Do they use it in their lives - if so when and if not why?
- How do they describe their identities?
- How would they describe London in terms of its identity?
- What do they think of diversity policies?

Of course, this was not a quantitative study. But a large majority of these young people distanced themselves from multiculturalism as they understood it, for a variety of different reasons. On the whole they said they preferred to use 'mixed' when describing certain 'multicultural' situations such as their educational institutions. And their reasons for being uncomfortable with, confused about or disinterested in what they take multiculturalism to mean were instructive.

## What does the term multiculturalism mean to them?

**There was a lack of clarity or interest among most.**

> 'I really don't use it. I prefer to say British'.
>
> *(Black female, 17)*

> 'It is so old-fashioned. My teachers will sometimes talk about festivals and that and we just laugh or yawn'.
>
> *(Asian female, 17)*

> 'It has nothing to do with our world. We don't sit around thinking oh this programme is really, really interesting because, hey, there is a black person in it. My friends are like all sorts. They are my mates'.
>
> *(White male, 19)*

> 'To be honest, I think this is something for sad old people'.
>
> *(Black male, 20)*

**Some robust reasons were also given by a minority about why they did not approve of the term.**

**Some, because multiculturalism seems shallow or irrelevant.**

> 'And I hate it when bloody politicians start talking about it before elections and bring in people like Trevor Phillips to show how multicultural they are'.
>
> *(Asian female, 18)*

> 'I think it is a stupid word used for black people when white people think they want to be polite'.
>
> *(Black male, 18)*

*'It's those bhangra bands and television geeks like Sayyid Jaffrey. I say I am British Asian and internationalist. Don't throw me your pitiful multicultchis'.*

*(Asian male, 20)*

**Nearly all of the respondents spoke positively about diversity, but two white respondents strongly disagreed.**

*'They have just taken over our city. Every chippie is run by a darkie or a Paki. I hate it. We all go to all-white pubs and clubs. They are all criminals and since this Lawrence kid, they are given everything. It's blacks who commit crime in London. Full Stop'.*

*(White male, 19)*

*'My friend was raped in Kilburn by a gang of black kids. They don't treat that as racist do they? I hate how they have moved into every part of London, even the nice areas like'.*

*(White female, 18)*

**Some respondents felt that multiculturalism was a soft option, taking the edge away from radical group-based politics.**

*'I am a proud British Muslim. I am close to my community and they are really proud that I am training to be a doctor. I would never give up that heritage. I feel I have nothing in common with all this multicultural stuff. Where were all these black brothers and sisters when we were being attacked over Rushdie? Did the CRE say anything to support us? My links are international. We are developing a modern, cosmopolitan Islamic network across the world'.*

*(Muslim female, 20)*

'I don't know. I am proud to be the son of an immigrant who came from Trinidad. But I am not an African-Caribbean. I am Black British, with very radical ideas about what that means. It means thinking you have a fundamental right to demand your place. Not beg for it like the older generations. So if the schools don't deliver, set up our own schools and make them the best there is. I hate that soppy nothing multicultural business. I have nothing in common with the Asian or white cultures'.

*(Black female, 20)*

**Others that multiculturalism was not inclusive and left them out.**

'It gives special treatment to those who are not white. We are all mixed in our cultures. My dad he is Polish. But I am not allowed to say that. If I say it I am called a racist'.

*(White female, 17)*

'Are Jews included? No. Are the English included? No. Would Shami Ahmed say that he is a multicultural success? No'.

*(Asian-White female, 19)*

'It's a boring word. It is grey and small and domestic. It does not include Europeans. It does not really include the world. It is like an old cardigan knitted out of different coloured scraps of wool'.

*(Asian male, 20)*

**But two interviewees thought it was a useful concept.**

'I belong to the school council and I think it is important if you want to change policies. People understand the word and you can make them feel guilty for not doing enough'.

*(Asian female, 17)*

*'For me it is a good word because it accepts that we have made a difference. Our food and music and all'.*

*(Asian female 18)*

## How did they describe their own identities and lifestyles?

**Some are unselfconsciously hybrid and open to diversity.**

*'I think of myself as a citizen of the world. That what we all are. Our lives are completely connected up now with the Internet. Would you ever describe the technological revolution as multicultural? I wear Paul Smith. I eat parathas cooked by my mum. I love cooking Chinese food myself. I want to work in Hong Kong'.*

*(Asian male, 20)*

*'I am in love with an Asian woman who is older than I am. She is gorgeous. She wears the shortest skirts in the kingdom. As the song should say, what's multiculturalism got to do with it?'*

*(White male, 20)*

*'Think Millie, the young mixed race lawyer in This Life. And that's my life. My mum is French and my dad is from South India. My sister has a child who is half-Senegalese. Most of my friends are young white law students who don't give a damn about my cultural background but who like me – individual free-thinking me'.*

*(Mixed-race female, 21)*

**Others are still in the process of negotiating this,**

*'I change my label many times in the day. One minute I am a young Brit who is keen on clubbing and cannabis. At home I am a dutiful Asian son who will join the family firm one day, though I can't see myself living like my dad and uncles. I love a good time too much. I also feel very much a part of Europe and would like my children to learn French. At college they see me as their great brown hope in squash'.*

(Asian male, 20)

**or feel that the assumptions of multiculturalism constrain them.**

*'If you come from an ethnic background, you are supposed to like particular things. I'm not into reggae – but it doesn't mean I can't be black, British and Jamaican'.*

(Black male, 20)

**Still others feel that multiculturalism is a barrier to real progress.**

*'I think, when I think of multiculturalism, I think of all the things which divide us and which we then have to tolerate, to be kind. The reality is that although some young people do act in tribes, most of us think we have much more in common than we are allowed to believe'.*

(Asian female, 18)

'I feel I am at the start of something different. I feel myself to be English ethnic for the first time in my life. I want to share in the pride all of us must feel in our backgrounds. And I want to imagine a country where we are a rainbow nation'.

(White male, 19)

'I am treated like a 'Paki' by immigration people – and by my own family as well. I resent the way my parents don't think I should want to be British at all. But I reject their traditions'.

(Asian female, 19)

## London and the identity of London

The majority of the interviewees felt positive about what the city was, but most said that the word multiculturalism was an inadequate description of the essence of the city as it now was.

'We are living in a throbbing city where the globe is here at our feet. In any one week I will be dealing with at least fifty different nationalities from here. I think we seriously need to get rid of that ridiculous old CRE way of thinking about who we are'.

(Black male, 19)

'I think it is sad that many trendy places are still so white. But that is about equality not about multi-culturalism. I think London is fantastic because it is so mixed, not because of that ugly palace or royal family. And it belongs to us, those of us who don't want to be one-dimensional. I would say that we have moved from old-fashioned multiculturalism to something much more positive'.

(Mixed-race male 21)

'I hate it when you still get white journalists and food critics judging our food and exploring our areas like we are some undiscovered tribes. In that sense I feel very possessive of my culture especially as they just take things from us. Instead of promoting our chefs they steal our food and make money writing their own books. Multiculturalism is just another kind of imperialism. But what I do know is that once upon a time living in Southall was depressing and frightening. Today it is the soul food of modern London'.

(Asian male, 20)

## Diversity Policies

**Most of the interviewees felt alienated by these policies.**

'I think it is rude that we have had all this multicultural programming and actually the media still gives a white view. Education is the same. I never watch East or Black Britain. I watch the news and Question Time. And what do I see? The world with white blinkers'.

(Black male, 22)

'I think it is right to ask that we should all be in there and up there. But I hate it when we are put into a box. I spend a lot of my time with other Asians. And I do love the Asian programmes. But I think the time has come to think differently. This has not helped us to change and develop'.

(Asian female, 19)

'Why do we need diversity policies for us and not the Italians who have been here for as long?'

(Muslim female, 20)

*'Most of my friends are white or mixed-race and I feel embarrassed that I have to get special treatment. It is unfair. And anyway we are all becoming more and more American. So how does that fit into multiculturalism?'*
*(Mixed-race female, 18)*

**For others, such policies are seen as an important stage in the fight for equality.**

*'Like I know my mum, she is a lawyer and she thinks that things are really changing in her profession because of an awareness of multiculturalism. She is in an all-white firm and people are more open to equal opportunities and diversity. But for me I think if they haven't got it yet, after the Lawrence case, then they don't want to accept us. So maybe much harder laws or something are needed to go hand in hand with diversity policies.'*
*(Black female, 19)*

*'I know that when I am a doctor I will have a fight to get to the top. In this profession there is little idea of even basic multiculturalism. Do you think consultants worry about it? So we mustn't throw out the idea of difference, although we should make it something more exciting and inclusive.'*
*(Muslim female, 20)*

For many of these young Britons, the idea of multiculturalism as used by journalists, academics, writers, politicians, community and religious spokespeople is old-fashioned, incomplete, static and divisive. It simply cannot explain or describe the complexity of what has happened to British society. Multiculturalism seems to have lost the lucidity and excitement it might once have had. Multiculturalism has always been used in an enclosed, limited way. Partly this was intended to make white people feel safe, because their world was only being minimally affected – but in fact they have felt excluded, leading to new tensions. And while multiculturalism intended to enhance the status and opportunities of new Britons, members of so-called 'ethnic minorities' have felt boxed in and constrained by the outdated assumptions it seems to make about who they are, what they want out of life and how we all fit together. If we are to deal with the wide range of responses – from optimistic internationalism, increasing separatism, rejection, apathy – it will not be enough to update multiculturalism. We need an approach which can capture many of the things which multiculturalism leaves out.

# 4. The many flavours of British multiculturalism – and why they fail

Any credible critique must recognise that there are many multiculturalisms, not a single approach. A wide range of different approaches are now part of our landscape – and have been adopted and promoted by business, local and health authorities, the equalities agencies, the voluntary sector, black and Asian groups, and individuals. Some of these may provide some of the foundations for a new approach. But, more often, they do not. For they are all severely limited and may even be creating new problems.

We will see that these many multiculturalisms can be broadly grouped into three sets – those which are minimalist and cautious, those which are positive and celebratory, and those which favour much more assertive group-based action. With so many multiculturalisms out there and on offer, one response might be that all is well – there seems to be a multiculturalism for everybody. But each of these forms of multiculturalism contains deep, perhaps fatal, flaws – and is too often seen as end in itself. And what is even more worrying is that the way in which they interact – or, more often, fail to do so – makes the problems and confusions greater still. So let us look at the different forms of multiculturalism which we are dealing with today.

## Consumer Multiculturalism

For a good many Britons, multiculturalism is simply a shallow celebration of different goods and forms of entertainment to satisfy an insatiable need for more things to consume. Compared with our purist European partners, Britons have found it easy and exciting to embrace the multiculturalism of curry clubs, Bob Marley and Pashmina shawls. Ironically, those with the reputation for being the warmest Europeans – Italians for example – seem to have developed the most fundamentalist tendencies when it comes to cultural purity. They will not eat the food of others; they would never experiment and change their own ways of doing things because they consider their own ways so superior to any others around the world. Britons have been more open to change. Some call this 'boutique' multiculturalism – which loves to pick in and out of difference without making a difference. Although this is the weakest of all the forms of multiculturalism, there has been a hearty approval of the increase of choice and pleasure that this form of multiculturalism has injected into the previously grey areas of life.

## Sexual Multiculturalism

The second version of multiculturalism also involves the desires and again Britain seemed to have found this form much more attractive than the rest of the European Union countries. Britain now has one of the highest rates of interracial relationships anywhere in the western world. A phenomenon which exercised Shakespeare – the issue is dealt with both in Othello and Titus Andronicus – has become one of the central, defining characteristics of modern Britain. The figures are astonishing. Nearly half of black men and a third of black women, and just under 15% of Asian men and 8% of Asian women, have a white partner. 40% of Afro-Caribbean children under the age of sixteen have one white parent.[9] New evidence shows that, over the centuries, the pre-twentieth century black populations were absorbed into the wider population. Genetically, it appears, one out of five modern Britons are their descendants. This trend is now unstoppable making it genetically impossible for this country ever to return to a myth of purity. These statistics then translate into real life transformations. Recently, an Asian wife of a prominent white writer was tragically killed at a very young age. At her funeral, a series of profoundly moving speakers spoke of how the world-view of her husband was completely transformed through this marriage.

## Artistic multiculturalism

The cultural loot in our museums – Chinese porcelain and painted silks, bronze Indian sculptures, Moghul miniature paintings, 'primitive' African art and countless books, including many of the oldest Korans in the world – bears ample testimony to the long history of adoration of non-Eurocentric writers, painters and art. When British sailors and explorers first set out in search of new goods and new worlds, they often came back with artefacts from those other cultures which the ruling powers defined as 'uncivilised'. Artistic inspiration too has been multicultural for centuries in this country. Think of the impact of other civilisations on Byron or EM Forster, the Pre-Raphaelites and William Morris. In modern times these forms of multiculturalism have moved from being acquisitive and in that sense consumerist to being a site of cultural production. Anish Kapoor, Chris Ofili, Salman Rushdie, Hanif Kureshi, Meera Syal and Steve McQueen have become British cultural products as well as sources of exciting new creativity. The old world has gained through the injection of new blood and, instead of appropriating the works of art, the artists and writers themselves have been incorporated into that vast British cultural industry.

## Style Multiculturalism

Fashion and youth culture have shown how images of diversity can be a selling point. Undyingly trendy, this form would, for example, apply to Channel Four television, which likes to promote a view of itself as non-traditional, non-fusty, libertarian, fast and iconoclastic. You are more likely, for example, to see stand-up black comedians who break all the rules on this channel. This is the channel which gave us a programme of young black men involved in gang rape activities as a hobby, or Badass TV which simply shows black people behaving badly and having a great time. The Ali G phenomenon – a Jewish man pretending to be a 'wigger', a white man wanting to be black – is another example. In fashion, designers like Hussain Chalayan are amongst the trendiest and most sought after today. Their styles are clearly influenced by their cultural backgrounds – but their market is the usual haute couture crowd. Pop music leads on this version of multiculturalism. Understanding well, the economic gains to be made by demolishing any barriers to talent, this industry (although there is still substantial discrimination against black and Asian artists) is able to see the turn-on factor in having mixed pop groups and black and Asian stars.

## Corporate Multiculturalism

Business has learnt from style multiculturalism that it too can market itself through multicultural imagery. Perhaps best represented by the bright and iconoclastic tail-fins adopted by British Airways a few years ago, this kind of multiculturalism is closely tied to globalisation and internationalism. Domestically this has meant a revolution in the way catalogues are now designed. Mothercare, Marks & Spencer, Argos all use the images of black, Asian and white Britons to represent and entice a cross-range of clients. Since the visible minorities in this country have spending power of around £40 billion pounds a year, this is an important marketing move. And this imagery has a much broader appeal. The booming food industry largely rests on this form of multiculturalism. Star chefs, start-up restaurants, TV food programmes and ready food industries thrive on the diversity of foods – curries, chinese food, pasta – which are now more British than Yorkshire pudding.

## Role Model Multiculturalism

These successes have led to a new form of multiculturalism much favoured by successful black people and by equalities agencies. The Commission for Racial Equality is increasingly promoting the positive contributions of black and Asian Britons as a useful counterforce to the negative image of immigration (usually referring to people who are not white) through the centuries in this country. A message is given to society that black and Asian people are worthy of their respect because many have earned it. And it is indisputable that the success of high-profile people such as Trevor MacDonald, Linford Christie, Kathy Tyson, Paul Boateng, Dianne Abbott and Gary Younge have influenced the aspirations of young Britons and challenged the idea that black and Asian people are a problem. By breaking through to the top echelons of the professions, and other areas, these successful people change expectations about who actors, journalists, newsreaders or MPs are – and have much more profound if diffuse effects on society's self-image.

## Geographical Multiculturalism

This form of multiculturalism is understood primarily in spatial terms. Cultural mixing is seen as a feature of, and problem for, our cities, and in particular London. This is of course accurate in one sense, if you understand multiculturalism to mean only the physical presence of non-white Britons. In areas such as Newham, Hackney and Southall between thirty and sixty percent of local populations are black or Asian. By definition therefore the areas are multiethnic and multicul-tural. Whether it is through the route of equal opportunities or the dynamics of market forces, this puts unavoidable pres-sures on those providing goods and services – in the public or private sectors – to respond to the diversity of the population. You can see it working. If you go to Alperton in West London, where there is a significantly large Asian population served by dozens of local Asian traders, you notice that the big Sainsburys superstore stocks a large variety of items which are intended to draw in an Asian clientele. The foods are more authentic, there is a greater variety and the sales pitch is targeted at those who are experts. But, according to this view, outside these geographical hotspots, multiculturalism has much less impact or relevance.

## Token multiculturalism

This links to a multiculturalism of an unspoken kind, much favoured by many liberals, who believe that, as long as you do a certain minimal amount – a few programmes on race on Radio 4, for example – you can carry on perpetuating white privilege and white values. The BBC is very keen on local, 'ethnic' stations, but not a single one of the defining voices of Radio 4 is black or Asian. Even more extraordinarily, Radio 1 and Radio 5 Live are also overwhelmingly white. The National Health Service would collapse without the 26 per-cent of Asian doctors and huge battalions of black and Asian nurses. But these people are underrepresented in positions of power – are they thought not good enough to be consultants or trust managers?

## Wishful multiculturalism

This has been based on the assumption that evolutionary processes will, in due course, see things right. People who argue this also tend to believe that it is perfectly understand-able why many white Britons have not been able to embrace multiculturalism thus far: they are only responding in a natural way to outsiders. Change, for those who hold this view, will only come with time as the children grow up together and drop the fear and suspicion between strangers. Much hope is invested in education – although there is often an uproar when schools do try and deliver any kind of meaningful changes to take account of diversity – but to try and hasten change is only likely to encourage a white backlash. This view is best encapsulated by the Telegraph's Paul Goodman:

"I think there are two completely different attitudes to time at work here. The people who arrive in the country as immigrants naturally want to make up time fast in modern times and find themselves quickly in positions of influence and responsibility and to have the opportunity and so on. Now you could do all that very quickly by fixing quotas say in certain industries or in institutions and so on. The problem is that this is essentially unfair because by seeking to do what some would call justice to one, you're doing an injustice to someone else. The other way of bringing about change is 'waiting for change to happen' ... the generations sort of go on, you go down to the third, fourth and fifth generations of those who originally arrived – you will find a growing identification with Britain's way of doing things. I think to try and create some kind of artificial, radical project is a route to disaster".[10]

## Numbers multiculturalism

But this idea that change will come about gradually, almost imperceptibly, is challenged by many who feel that issues of equity and fairness can not wait for their grandchildren's children. And so a counting heads understanding of multiculturalism has come to occupy the minds and policies of almost every public institution in the country, and increasing numbers of private businesses. The key tool of multiculturalism is seen as monitoring the ethnic background of the workforce. In fact, for many, multiculturalism has become the view that fairness to any group means ascribing an ethnic identity to each person, and then seeking to monitor all areas of life to check how far they reflect the percentages of different black and Asian communities. This has come about through a combination of organised pressure 'from below', from the media finding this an easy, simple measure of multiculturalism to apply, and through business, local government and political leaders realising the benefits of being seen to be taking issues of multiculturalism seriously in this way.

## Heritage multiculturalism

This is a form of multiculturalism, traditionally favoured by many post-war politicians, based on the belief that 'immigrants' are so peculiar, so different from mainstream British society that the only way to preserve good race relations is to permit these cultural villagers to live their own lives – and to carry on with their religious and cultural practices as long as they do not make too many demands on the state. And traditional members and 'leaders' of these 'immigrant communities' have found this most satisfying. This form of multiculturalism can slow down cultural change as it privileges those who seem to want to preserve an idea of, say, India or Jamaica which is no longer found in those countries themselves. Multiculturalism has also seen, and encouraged, a fragmenting of identities. Where once many people of colour were happy to call themselves black, we are now Asian, Hindu, Caribbean, African, Muslim, even Shia Muslims. This then gives us a platform for making demands which are not only positive, but negative, against other groups. Grassroot Muslim organisations claim that they are neither black nor Asian and must therefore have their own separate funding.

## So what's wrong with the multiculturalisms we have?

A number of these multiculturalisms overlap and reinforce each other. Others seem diametrically opposed. But these many multiculturalisms can be classified in three types. One set of approaches is broadly mimimalist – seeing multiculturalism as a marginal question where all will be well as long as we wait for the evolutionary process to take its course. Another is much more optimistic and believes that there is much to celebrate. The third seeks to promote much more assertive group-based action to speed the process up. But all of these approaches are simplified and incomplete. How can our 'coriander consumerism' tell us anything about what we should do about education or human rights? In fact, when it comes to dealing with the inevitable tensions between different multicultural approaches, we do not yet really have a shared framework for deciding what should be done in practice.

| Attitude to multiculturalism | Forms of multiculturalism |
|---|---|
| Minimalist | Wishful multiculturalism<br>Geographical multiculturalism<br>Token multiculturalism |
| Celebratory | Consumer multiculturalism<br>Sexual multiculturalism<br>Artistic multiculturalism<br>Style multiculturalism<br>Corporate multiculturalism |
| Tribal | Heritage multiculturalism<br>Numbers multiculturalism |

## Why minimalist multiculturalisms can't keep diversity in the box

The minimalist multiculturalisms claim that multiculturalism can be divided off by geography and ethnicity, and that these groups should be given due respect and the space to do a little of their own thing until they 'catch up' or their children change and dissolve into mainstream culture. This belief has underpinned much post-war understanding of multiculturalism on all sides. It implies that the multiculturalism debate can be largely ignored by mainstream society and that nothing much needs to be done. All will be well and all it will take is a little, or a lot of, time. The only risk is that we might upset this evolutionary process by doing too much, too soon. This discourse has always claimed that our 'excellent' race relations depend upon firm immigration controls because the country cannot be expected to 'tolerate' too much difference. The race equality laws, have, in a sense, been part of the deal that needed to be offered to 'ethnic minorities' to keep the peace.

But these approaches have failed because they were limited and ad hoc, not part of an overarching national strategy to get the country to move into a modern era. White Britons were failed historically by the political elite who did not prepare them for the changes that came after the war – and who still give out mixed messages about whether immigration has been a good thing for this nation. One moment people in Britain were being taught that they were the imperial masters who had the God-given responsibility to rule and civilise the barbarians they controlled – the next minute these black and Asian people were in the work canteen demanding to be treated as equals. White Britons were told that black and Asian immigration was a threat but at the same time they were instructed to treat those who were here as equals. One could argue that exactly the same muddle has prevailed over the way European integration was handled after 1970.

But, even though the elite was very slow to lead on this, the country has nevertheless been transformed. There is no corner in the United Kingdom which can claim to be homogeneous, 'traditional' and untouched by diversity. Complex spillovers and leakages come about through the kinds of interactions which could not have been predicted even thirty years ago.

## Why celebratory multiculturalisms fail to deliver

But the failures of minimalist multiculturalists to understand these changes does not mean that all will be well if we simply embrace and celebrate a shiny, new, shared 'hybridity'. The celebratory multiculturalisms – from football to fashion, the creative industries to enlightened corporations and the positive images promoted by the equality agencies – may sometimes provide useful correctives to fears about difference, but they do not encompass a deep understanding of what diversity means in a shared society.

There is a risk in seeming to sell multiculturalism as a trend – which may prove shallow and temporary – and making easy success seem possible through the elevation of one or two individual stars like Scary Spice, Naomi Campbell or Ozwald Boateng. And, because celebrations of multiculturalism usually promote elite achievements, which many people do not think are relevant to their own lives, they can fail to connect with many people. Without a progressive vision of the values which should animate our shared society, simply telling positive stories about black and Asian Britons does not enable us to construct a framework to tackle the issues of social exclusion, to deal with racism or to understand the resentments of those who feel excluded from these new narratives. More seriously, telling society that black and Asian people are worthy of their respect because many have earned it is quite different from telling people that black and Asian people – good and bad, successful and unsuccessful – are an intrinsic part of this country and that they should have no additional pressure put on them to be good or do good than anyone else. A black prisoner is as much a part of British society as is Lenny Henry. And for every hero or heroine elevated, a demon lingers in the shadows. For every Frank Bruno, there is a Winston Silcott. This multicultural method implies that in spite of racism, in spite of injustice, those with the will can actually transcend their circumstances – something that is true of a few but not of the majority.

Celebratory multiculturalisms also tend to gloss over the tensions of cultural transfer and engagement. It is always fascinating to see how new battles over ownership and identity are played out. Once again, the battle for Salman Rushdie's soul has been one of the most illuminating episodes of recent times. A British Asian, passionately engaged in anti-racism, becomes reviled by his own. He has to decide where he belongs. He wavers and there is one moment when he nearly retreats and announces that he is re-joining his Muslim brethren. His white supporters are appalled at this 'betrayal' which turns out to be only a small moment of uncertainty. He defects back to them. So much of what Rushdie writes is inaccessible to most white readers, because it is Bombay slang and Islamic theology, yet since the storm over *The Satanic Verses*, he has been reclaimed by the white intellectual and artistic community as one of their sons. The battles over who black and Asian artists are – are they exotic and deliciously foreign or are they the new Brits – are constant and continuous. Not owning them makes Britain appear Eurocentric. When there is true acceptance, fears arise of appropriation, and there is always a painful distancing which has to take place between the successful artist or writer and the communities from which they first emerged. Celebratory multiculturalisms rarely capture or understand this. Even with sexual multiculturalism, it is the way in which we talk about it which is the problem. It may be that this apparently deepest, least rhetorical and most 'real' form of celebratory multiculturalism is sometimes the closest to the minimalist argument that we need not at all interfere with natural processes of social evolution – now that there are chocolate-coloured children and babies in ever-increasing numbers, all of the other problems will dissolve and disappear.

## Why tribal multiculturalisms do more harm than good

But attempts to create multiculturalisms with more teeth have often led us down blind alleys. These tribal multicul-turalisms do recognise difference. The problem is that they recognise little else. They may seem to have more bite than the celebratory forms – but they are often no less simplistic. At their worst, these forms of multiculturalism take differ-ences as essentialist and never-changing, and seek to divide people into separate and mutually exclusive categories which do not reflect either the complexities of our identities or the ways in which we must all interact deeply with each other in our shared society.

There has been a degree of dishonourable purpose in this laissez-faire method of multiculturalism. It makes few demands on leaders to change their view of Britishness or of cultural and political empowerment. In areas where the eth-nic vote matters, politicians can do well by deliberately not disturbing the cultural enclaves – in order to keep the tradi-tionalists happy and get their help in delivering black votes. Those with real power need to ensure that they engage with and tackle these issues of social exclusion – especially when they can clearly lead to human rights abuses.

This form of multiculturalism also tends to fossilise the idea of culture. Traditional advocates of multiculturalism have been slow to move their thinking to accommodate the changes which are taking place in the most conservative of communities. Few British Muslim women, old or young, would freely move to an Islamic country if they had to sur-render the basic autonomy which most have acquired in this country. Today the 'A' level participation rate of Muslim girls is higher than that of white boys. Black women are getting much more ambitious and competing at the highest levels and in effect challenging the cultural stereotype of the victim locked in double jeopardy. Bhikhu Parekh is right to point out that "in every family husband and wife, parents and children, brothers and sisters are having to re-negotiate and re-define their patterns of relationships in a manner that takes into account both their traditional values and the characteristics of their adopted country. Different families reach their own, tentative solutions".[11] This is culture on the move, not culture preserved lovingly in a jewellery box.

As these discussions are played out within and between groups, there has been growing support within all groups for the idea that all cultures living in the nation should submit to the basic principles of human rights and equality – and that difference is only acceptable if it does not fail this test. Yet those who advocate this model, perhaps the most workable of all, are seen as a threat to cultural autonomy by many who claim the multicultural banner. But the increasing balkanising of identities has real and damaging effects. Young black and Asian people are forming gangs and attacking each other in schools and the streets, even those whose parents are long time friends. And some of the more militant Islamic groups around the world are seeking recruits among Muslim students on British campuses.[12]

While most of us would be very uncomfortable about dividing our society up into ever smaller tribes, almost all of us do participate in a milder version of the same approach, playing the numbers game to find out how multicultural any of us, or our institutions, are. Of course tackling discrimination and barriers to opportunities are important – and monitoring numbers can be one indicator of that. But the impact of this idea of what the multiculturalisation of a workplace means remains an act of faith. There is little evidence to show that changing the ethnic composition of the workforce itself genuinely changes the values within an establishment, whether those at the receiving end of services perceive that an important shift has taken place in the way that services are delivered, or indeed whether such a change is perceived as positive. The hidden assumption is that only black people can promote a culture of equality and diversity – and that they do this by being there. Some may not want to have this burden in their professional lives. Others may feel that this allows white people off the hook.

And it does mean that diversity remains firmly a minority question – instead of rethinking the overall approach and values of these organisations, and how their output reflects the society we think we are today. Similarly, in the arts field, if funders have the view that they must allocate a certain percentage of their resources to the 'ethnics' there is never any danger of major transformations of what the National Theatre should stand for – to examine how much is being done to move away from the Eurocentric tendencies of the theatre world to a global vision. It is also revealing that newspapers such as *The Guardian* and *The Independent*, which have not been as positive as one might have expected in terms of employment, do now cover issues to do with the changing nature of this country with superb insight. This is actually greater progress than having black people who have been brought in to carry the burden of anti-racism and multiculturalism, a point that was well made by Herman Ouseley, in his last interview before he left his post as chairperson of the Commission for Racial Equality. While discussing the racial composition of the Greater London Assembly he said "I believe an all-white authority can be forced to deliver equality. A lot of black people have said to me 'I don't care who they are. In fact, if they are white and they are doing it right, I will support them more than if they are black and not doing the business'.[13]

## Multiculturalism and its enemies

There have always been differences between competing and incomplete forms of multiculturalism. But it is important that we now engage fully in this debate and sort out what we want our shared and diverse identities to be and mean. At precisely the time when issues of cultural identity are becoming central to British politics as rarely before, traditional multiculturalism doesn't any longer have the resources to defeat its enemies in public debate. Multiculturalism may, in fact, contain the seeds of its own destruction because it too often concedes the vital ground to its opponents. A bastardised form of the traditional multicultural agenda has been largely hijacked and put to non-progressive ends – making it increasingly a force for division, not cohesion. Meanwhile, and partly in response, the traditional enemies of multiculturalism have resurfaced in new multicultural clothing – having realised that they can employ what they understand to be multicultural resources and arguments effectively in their own cause. A very angry representative of the Countryside Alliance told Andrew Marr that his folk were the new despised minority in this 'multicultural' society.[14] In 1999 the Commission of Racial Equality had a number of complaints from English Britons complaining about discrimination against them by the Scots. It is difficult to see how multiculturalism can respond unless we can replace it with something entirely different – which can understand the forces of anxiety which drive the emerging identity politics of Asians, blacks and whites alike, but which can also find the resources to go beyond these by providing a new coherent identity and narrative.

## The 'enemies within'

In the UK, anti-multiculturalisms have taken many different forms. Because of the assumption that multiculturalism was a black and Asian thing – making all blacks and Asians somehow part of the multicultural coalition – many of its fiercest radical black critics have been seen as 'enemies within'. In fact, these critics had always regarded multiculturalism as fundamentally flawed and a treacherous soft option.

The radical preference has always been for anti-racism which they say addresses the central problem of structural inequality and power. The Institute for Race Relations, for example, under the passionate leadership of A. Sivananden, has consistently said that the problem is not difference but oppression and that multiculturalism has been used as a sop by the state to diffuse the energy of black Britons.[15] The police failures in the Stephen Lawrence case, following twenty years of 'cultural sensitivity' training, did not come from a lack of multicultural awareness. The Lawrences are culturally no different from the Smiths and Jones. But they were treated as second class citizens because of racist assumptions and behaviour. However, many of these radical black intellectuals have undervalued and misunderstood the importance of culture and identity – and have been excessively reductive in their approach. And those today who articulate increasingly disaggregated black and Asian identities often draw upon similar arguments – but now claim to be promoting, developing and radicalising multiculturalism itself. The dangers are that individuals are expected to subscribe to a single-dimensional and much narrower identity than most of us have or want, and that the extension of this approach threatens to break up our society into separate enclaves – dealing with everything from ethics to education – with far too little to collectively bind us together.

## White flight and fight – and the new white multiculturalism

And perhaps the biggest reason why multiculturalism never really connected in the way that was needed was that it has always seemed to leave most white people – and so most people in this country – out. This is no longer possible. One of the most illuminating programmes on British television in recent times was the Channel 4 series *White Tribe* presented by Darcus Howe, who went round the country in search of the English identity. You watched white people from around the country rejecting multiculturalism as they understand it. Some were obviously determined racists, others were confused. They spoke fearfully and furiously of not being allowed to be white or discuss their anxieties. They saw black people as unfairly advantaged because they were part of the multicultural kingdom. Yet the genesis of this remarkable series itself illustrates the deficiencies of present-day British multiculturalism. Narinder Minhas, the series producer, could not sell this idea to television commissioning editors: "They could see that there was a need for multicultural output but were locked into old ways of thinking. For them, multiculturalism meant programmes made for black people by black people about black subjects".[16]

Young white people are also expressing a worrying set of attitudes. In a powerful and disturbing study carried out in 1996, the academic Roger Hewitt examined the attitudes of young racist thugs in Greenwich, the area where teenagers Stephen Lawrence, Rohit Duggal and Rolan Adams were killed in racist attacks. He found that there is more mature awareness of what it means to live in a multi-ethnic society but that this has made extreme racism worse in certain neighbourhoods. The Howe programmes and this research revealed a 'radical new theme' emerging with increasing numbers of white people claiming that black people are getting all the attention. In 1997, the European Youth Survey published by MTV found that young white Britons (16-24 year olds) were the most racist in Europe. 30% disagreed that all races and cultures are equal – compared to 19% in Germany – and 26% said they would never date anyone who was of a different colour.[17] Many of these people were born into multiculturalism and educated within it – yet they have emerged as violently hostile to diversity.

At school in particular, white children have been alienated by the way multiculturalism was played out, where all previously colonised societies were uncritically 'celebrated' and white civilisations implicitly accused and undermined. There is essential work to be done on providing a more relevant and inclusive curricula but you do not redress past injustices by inflicting guilt on or diminishing those who are three generations removed from those who were responsible. But that is what happened in far too many cases. As Hewitt says: "White pupils, to some extent, seem like cultural ghosts, haunting as mere absences the richly decorated corridors of multicultural societies".[18] In an ironic twist, some of those who have most resented multiculturalism now use the arguments perfected by multiculturalists to demand their fair share.

The right in Europe is busy cashing in on the enormous anxiety felt by many Europeans by building its politics on this paranoia. Leaders are fostering resentment against the 'other' – usually non-white people who are (with impunity) described as economic parasites or a cultural contagion. The US is increasingly dominant in the global economy, and continues to assert its might in international politics, but the majority of its people remain inward-looking, wilfully ignorant of other countries, always prone to isolationism. Britain is particularly susceptible, because of the ubiquity of the English language and because all those institutions and ideas which anchored this nation for so long – the monarchy, and the class structure, for example – are losing their grip.[19] Some Conservatives in Britain, frustrated by their loss of power, are gathering to offer the safe old option, a return back to the future where modern economic change is 'managed' through invocations of old values, the Empire and Europhobia. The great free-marketeers and privatising Tories could not stomach British Airways using myriad images instead of the

Union Jack, as Mrs Thatcher memorably showed. But there is no going back – we can not simply put a handkerchief over the present and look away.

In all sorts of ways in our society, these 'multicultural' interactions can not be avoided – most obviously in the close proximity, mixed schools and streets make it impossible even to dream of whiter times. But in many localities, such as is the case on some housing estates in the East End of London, the desire is for each group to keep to itself as far as is possible, and the interactions are too often conflictual and borne out of resentment and competition for scant resources. Multiculturalism, from the white point of view, then becomes a curse, a terrible imposition on people who believe that before such times, their country was truly plentiful and safe. Criminality, bad schooling, poor housing are all seen as the fault of multiculturalism. In middle class areas, there is also evidence of 'flight' away from diversity, particularly when it comes to schooling, and a reluctance to mix. And in areas of geographical proximity where children may share schools, there is still a marked reluctance from many on all sides to encourage further involvement. When many of our forms of multiculturalism have been built on the premise that 'immigrants' are so peculiar, so different from mainstream British society that the only we can live together is if we keep apart just as much as is possible, it is perhaps unsurprising that they are failing to enable us to deal with the society we live in today.

So we need to develop skills and imagination which can extend our understanding of a diverse and shared society. Take the example of the English at present. Can they not see that the anxieties that they are going through about their ethnicity in many ways replicate the feelings of Hindus in Leicester and Muslims in Bradford? The questions troubling them all are the same. How much can they surrender their deeply felt ethnic, historic or religious identities for the sake of some other broader and more dominating culture? How do they maintain an ancestral connection with their past and still feel easy in this brave new multifarious world?

# Part Two

# After Multiculturalism

# 5. The New Approach

After multiculturalism, we need to collectively reimagine ourselves and our society, recognising both our diversity and our collective resources – so that we are enabled and prepared for a very different world from that which multiculturalism was created to serve. This is not an assimilationist argument – an ideology which has failed even in the United States and which harks back to an age of monolithic and controlled identities, when it is multiple identities and the ability to use them flexibly which are the essential tools for coping with the complexities of modern life today. But nor is this an ode to thoughtless and limitless diversity, which only ends up dividing peole even within neighbourhoods. Different cultures are to be valued but it is always wrong for them to take precedence over fundamental human rights. While it is important that we respect and celebrate cultural difference, we should not idealise or fossilise different cultures or punish people who can not live within narrow constraints.

For we are never again, thanks to the communications revolution, ever going to be able to retreat into our own neatly fenced-off and severely protected boundaries. Global business alone will make this impossible. We need to understand how changes in capitalism enable the making of immeasurable economic gains but can also exacerbate global inequalities and create fears of a loss of control and self-determination, even of cultural annihilation – fears which are all the greater because there is no escape from this force. We can not avoid the fact that globalisation is transforming us, our lives, our identities and the way in which we think about the world. Foreign investment in Britain has gone up from £10 billion in 1979 to £415 billion in 1997 while British investments abroad have grown from £21.6 billion to £574 billion. And the social and cultural changes are often even greater. As Andrew Marr says "Global power is inside the products that are inside our houses and inside the computer web that is now inside our heads ... whether it is about management skills, capital, technology or branding, patriotism takes second place to quality".[20]

If we are not just to cope with globalisation but to take these opportunities to enhance our lives, and find the resources to deal collectively with the new problems and new anxieties which are thrown up, then we will need to find a genuinely exciting alternative to ethnocentric nationalism and particularistic multiculturalism. This will need to help us all to embrace Europe and feel at ease in the world, to provide new coherence to our society while understanding diversity and dealing with it fairly. This will make demands of black, Asian and, now increasingly, white Britons to emerge from their enclaves and have their cultures interrogated in the national and international arena.

## New narratives to unite – stories to connect and to liberate

But the needs of patriotism cannot be ignored in this fast-moving world, which often provides the very conditions which lead to malign developments. There is an acute need to reimagine the British nation, especially in these post – devolution and global times when the integrity of this nation state is under severe pressure. As Linda Colley says, the internet, migration, e-commerce and growing global links in culture, economics and politics may be exciting but they "also represent an assault on all kinds of customary boundaries, beliefs and allegiances".[21]

The old British identity is indeed passing away as Marr has memorably said. So what is to take its place? We can attempt valiantly to revive it, we can mark this passing and then concentrate on local identities and Europe, or we can make a vibrant new Britishness in which diversity is at the heart and not in the toenails of the body politic. But we can't just muddle through, as an "asymmetrical state full of different but inchoate allegiances"[22] – we need something more substantial to re-connect us. And so internationalists and social democrats have got to find a way of responding which allows for all to be rooted and which rejuvenates the national spirit, with a deeper attachment to our European future and a sense of global connectedness underpinned by ideals of human rights and justice.

Many remarkable writers have already shown that a national identity is created mostly through myth-making. It is much more than a territory, a political entity or historical accident. It has a subjective existence with beliefs, traditions and self understanding. The right believes that these can only be known intimately and unselfconsciously by those on the inside and can never be accessible to those across the boundaries – imagined or real, internal or external – except in the most superficial way. This regenerative project has already been initiated in the United States by enlightened people. Berkley Professor Ron Takaki in his excellent book, *A Different Mirror* asks: "Will Americans of diverse races and ethnicities be able to connect themselves to a larger narrative? Whatever happens we can be sure that much of our society's future will be influenced by which 'mirror' we see ourselves".[23] Americans need more than ever before to understand that, in order to be whole, they must see themselves as members of humanity as well as one nation. He goes on to say "While our stories contain the memories of different communities, together they describe a larger narrative. Filled with what Walt Whitman celebrated as the 'varied carols' of

America, our denied history bursts with telling".[24] And we in Britain need these ties that bind even more since we have no active written constitution, nor flag – worshipping tendencies. Here the challenge is to bind and enthuse by fundamentally rethinking notions of heritage, belonging and greatness. As the critic Maya Jaggi says "Cultural heritage is widely seen as an embodiment of the spirit of a nation, part of the cement of a national identity for what is after all an 'imagined community'".[25]

Instead of saying that Britain has become a multicultural country since the war and that we should learn to 'tolerate' difference, people need to take pride in the fact that Britain has always been a country ready to embrace difference throughout history – albeit sometimes through control and acquisition. Muslims did not arrive here after the 1950s but have been here since the 1550s and brought with them (four centuries before Starbucks) the idea of the slowly drunk coffee in affable coffee houses.[26] The novelist Caryl Phillips writes in his introduction to the anthology *Extravagant Strangers: A Literature of Belonging,* "Britain has developed a vision of herself as a nation that is both culturally and ethnically homogeneous, and this vision has made it difficult for some Britons to feel that they have the right to participate fully in the main narrative of British life".[27] The empire needs to be described now beyond the post-colonial impasse. Mainstream British society has never properly acknowledged the damage which colonialism inflicted – but black and Asian Britons on the other hand have never allowed themselves to examine how their forebears were also often implicated in the project, nor what the gains were. After all, how could 10,000 Brits control India on their own? Some developments illustrate what can and must be done. The museum recording the impact of the slave trade on Liverpool is finally making that city come to terms with its own history and the highly rated Channel Four series on the history of slavery, which exposed the gains made by this country and also the part played by Africans, was a milestone because it challenged both white and black denials about this central historical crime.

The whole notion of heritage as understood by conservatives such as Roger Scruton comes into question once this invisible history is instated. As Stuart Hall said in a momentous lecture he delivered at a major Arts Council conference debating this very issue: "Like personal memory, social memory is highly selective. It highlights and foregrounds, imposes beginnings, middles and ends on the random and contingent. But equally it foreshortens, silences, disavows, forgets and elides many episodes which – from another perspective – could be the start of a different narrative. Despite this, the process of selective 'canonisation' confers authority and a material and institutional facticity, making it extremely difficult to shift or revise".[28]

## A society of values, not a non-interference pact

This vision is completely different from the old domestic multiculturalism and has serious implications for Black and Asian Britons. 16 million Muslims in Europe cannot be in Europe and not of it. They need to change and move from their mindset which tells them that they are a 'minority' with no other relationship with the mainland. In the European context, we are all 'minorities' now. The walls between groups must always have windows and doors capable of being opened. No group has special privileges, but no groups can claim special dispensations and opt-outs either. The narrow meanings of 'multiculturalisms' have no place in a country where neighbourhoods suddenly find that the Japanese (rich, and much needed for the wealth and jobs they create) are as much part of this landscape as newly arrived destitute Bosnians. Black and Asian Britons gain nothing from protecting their own multicultural spaces from these new arrivals.

British multiculturalism has never adequately debated the

tensions between equality, cultural rights and individual free-doms. Kymlicka describes these as the pressure between groups demanding external protection but being called to account for any internal oppression of their own which is often excused on the grounds of multiculturalism. Take the issue of forced marriages, for instance. When families and communities are confronted by people who wish to eradicate this practice because it violates the basic human rights of individuals, they are always accused of being assimilationist and against multiculturalism. Stuart Hall is right to argue that this is a necessary conversation that has yet to take place within groups and between them: "The depth of commitment of Britain to liberal values is not going to wither away just because there are different people around...so we have to argue about this. We might have to work against the grain of the system and say that individuals do have the right to live their lives from within, to exit, to write their own scripts, but within a broader recognition in public and not just in private of the differences which now constitute British society, a kind of loose weave notion of that society".[29]

It may be, in fact, that libertarian moral relativism – 'every-one's got the right to their opinion' – 'who's to say that we're right and they're wrong' – provides a muddled reason for a wider acceptance of multicultural tolerance. But no society can actually function without ethical foundations. Progressive people need to promote the view that this island belongs to everyone and that it is confident enough to progress devolu-tion and feel empowered by the ever changing demographic profiles and cultural inflows which are a condition of moder-nity. It is only the unimaginative or the uncourageous who fear this. But, for the centre to hold, there are binding values based on human rights and social responsibilities which apply to everyone. Those from societies which have unacceptably unequal gender roles will have to surrender these for the greater good. Those with an inflated view of their own greatness will have to do the same. There will be a recognition that fundamentalist secular liberalism, based entirely on individual rights and freedoms, diminishes too much the need for individuals to belong and believe and that social spaces must strive for integration and cross-fertilisation of ideas which can be interrogated by others. In short, there will be challenges for everybody and we need to show that there will also be collective gains from this.

## Dealing with exclusion, not numbers

Taking a more holistic approach to poverty and social exclusion has been one of the more impressive achievements of New Labour. An integrated strategy where race, ethnicity, gender and class discrimination are all considered in the diagnosis and, hopefully, solutions optimises the chances of long-term success. Although it is important never to take a colour-blind approach – because race and ethnicity do make an important difference to people's experiences and aspirations – it is important not to focus entirely on the racial minorities as if they are a breed apart. We know that poverty remains a problem and that the children of the poor have much worse health and education than the middle classes. We also know that Bangladeshis and Pakistanis are among the poorest Britons we have. A Social Exclusion and Inclusion model where the particularities of the non-white groups are incorporated is a more sensible response than 'race equality' measures which are often under-resourced and ineffectual.

There have been many mistakes made in the way local authorities have tried to intervene in impoverished and high-stress areas in the past. Selling superficial multiculturalism of the all-black sort to poor whites whose drains never work is only asking for black communities to be victimised and for a breakdown in community relations. This is partly what led to the killing of the white boy Richard Everitt by Bangladeshi youths in Somerstown in Camden in 1995 and what lies behind the quite appalling levels of racial violence against black and Asian people in the East End of London.

There are some good examples of how to create a sense of community among those with very little. Some authorities have encouraged neighbourhood festivals rather than 'multi-cultural' celebrations and, more concretely, involved the people living on estates much more in planning important changes to their environment rather than always assuming that the planners know best. These initiatives have brought diverse communities together to work on programmes producing some lasting benefits.

## Diversity as competitive edge, not woolly liberalism

And we also need to shed the image and approach of multi-culturalism as a worthy and passive project – which we *ought* to engage in but which often seems such hard work. We need to be clear that, from the child being taught in school to the business seeking to dominate the marketplace, only those who are comfortable with ubiquitous diversity and equipped to deal with it successfully will be able to thrive in the modern world. As Stuart Hall says, "The Brits owe this, not only to us, but to themselves: for to prepare their own people for success in a global and decentred world by continuing to misrepresent Britain as a closed, embattled, self-sufficient, defensive, 'tight little island' would be to fatally disable them".

This goes well beyond companies adjusting to the fact that so much business comes their way from the visible minorities in this country. Any sensible and ambitious business drive will accommodate and promote diversity – but that this does not mean treating this as a separate, niche market of people with different tastes, preferences and needs. Marks & Spencer is one of the most trusted companies for black and Asian Britons. Not only do they love the goods, they want to and do work for the firm in increasing numbers. Like Mothercare and Argos and many others, M&S use the images of black, Asian and white Britons to represent and entice a cross range of clients. But, like many other British firms, they have failed to capitalise fully on the opportunities to profit from the increased diversity in tastes of their customer base across the board. McDonalds' Indian and Chinese menus were aimed at everybody, not at specific ethnic groups. An M&S Shalwar Khameez which brings together high quality, modern British design and Asian styles would be a bestseller not only for British Asians but as much for young white men and women who do want to wear the clothes but feel too self-conscious going into Southall or Wembley.

The firms which are doing best in this environment are those which realise that it is not simply a case of hiring black and Asian employees to move towards a 'representative' workforce, but ensuring that the business takes advantage of all of the resources and skills available to it, in its shared and collective interest. In 2000, the outgoing Director General of the Institute of Directors, Tim Melville-Ross said: "All my experience tells me that organisations and the people who work in them prosper when inclusion is the watchword and discrimination is shown the door". Whereas the linguistic diversity of London, now greater than that in any other city in the world, has usually been discussed as a problem, a sign of backwardness, something which will hold schools and children back, it is now becoming clear that this is one important reason which multinational companies give for investing here. Certain oil companies have incorporated highly talented black and Asian individuals at management levels and many are called upon to play a useful part at the interface where they can draw on their own knowledge and background when there are local sensitivities and conflicts to be resolved. Highly qualified West Africans, for example, can be seen as an enormous asset by oil companies operating in Nigeria. In Hong Kong, and with increasing market openings in China, British Chinese economists and investment bankers are similarly proving to have additional skills which their employees can draw upon.

This a lesson which politics can learn – with the same goal of using all resources in the collective interest. The outdated discourse of 'ethnic minorities' has usually been about the problems for politics – whether education, crime or foreign policy. The American experience, where group mobilisation in politics is one of the rules of the game, has created a US-dominated academic discourse about diaspora communities in foreign policy which largely sees particular groups as a complication and a threat, likely to be a problem for foreign policy in particular. Japanese Americans – American citizens, including many who were American-born – were interned during world war two. The dominant fear has continued to be that diasporas will compete with and detract from the goals of the nation as a whole, with their own specific foreign policy interests and agenda. But this old-fashioned view can not take advantage of many of the foreign policy assets which this country has.

## Global involvement, not island multiculturalism

The central feature of this new approach will be that it will recognise that we no longer have boundaries of the mind which entirely match those of the nation. The need to engage deeply with others will be, and can not avoid being, an inter-nationalist approach, increasingly as Pico Iyer writes "to feel partially adjusted everywhere"[30] and to take responsibilities. Those running Red Nose Day show what can be achieved with this new awareness, while avoiding old stereotypes of dependence.

The BBC journalist Olenka Frankel makes controversial films about honour killings in Pakistan to get the world to notice and begin a process of change. Traditional multiculturalists accuse her of interfering in their culture – she argues that as a world citizen she has the right to intervene.[31] But I would go further and assert that she and others have no right not to intervene in these matters, provided such actions are not based on old imperialist notions of barbarism and where local people – in this case Pakistani women's groups – actually wish to get this worldwide publicity through a well resourced and respected organisation like the BBC. The problems of Kashmir are an important part of the portfolios of a number of British MPs who have many constituents from India and Pakistan. Concerns about Hong Kong, Nigeria, Uganda and Iran are similarly 'represented'. There are new and deep connections which go well beyond ideas about 'us and them' – the connections are now here, there and everywhere.

When we are involved in supporting democratisation and humanitarian action – from informal links right up to official military involvement, in cases like Bosnia and Kosovo – we need to connect this to who we are and what we stand for as a nation. Politicians need to ensure that they both explain and address the causes of conflict – to explain that it is a commitment to a stable international order which could help stem the tide of asylum-seekers, not speeches and leaflets that play on fears about being swamped.

This new internationalism will work if people here see it as rooted in Britain's global history, identity and responsibilities and if we show that we are responding to local concerns and needs. Robin Cook has argued that "the national interest is increasingly the international interest" – and we all need to understand that we can best serve our needs and interests by producing results that are beneficial globally. This goes far beyond ideas of elite cosmopolitanism – a hybrid, ultimately rootless culture which arose out of post-modernism and which is associated with globetrotting academics and businessmen, and which often fails to understand the basis on which its own, safe cosmopolitan world depends. Instead, a new approach would facilitate a deep involvement and engagement – with what Richard Weston calls the 'glocal' sensibility where local and global values are both competing and interlocking[32] and where the cosmopolitanism is rooted and attached in the way Nehru described. He once said that he was a committed internationalist because he was so securely rooted.

Unlike the cost-free celebratory multiculturalism which does not go beyond the rhetorical level, this has serious and powerful policy implications – from home affairs from immigration policy to citizenship, education and foreign policy – which I will examine out in the conclusion, and which are very different from the traditional multicultural instincts and approaches.

# 6. Conclusion: Going beyond multiculturalism in practice

Moving beyond multiculturalism means rethinking who we are as a nation, and changing the way we deal with very many policy areas as a result – because the underlying assumptions of many policy debates remain tied to the idea of a homogeneous white majority or to old-fashioned multiculturalism, both of which foster an outdated division between 'them and us'. We will need to rethink the assumptions behind policy across the board. In an era of holistic government, there should be no area of public life which is not affected. But major policy areas where change can begin include:

## Religious Diversity

*Traditional multiculturalism* proposes the path of least resistance to deal with the many anachronisms, protections and privileges which the Church of England receives. The familiar alliance between conservatives who want as little as possible to change and traditionalist leaders of minority communities is to extend many of these to many more, or to all, religions. The blasphemy laws would be extended to cover offences to many religions, which would also be represented by right in the House of Lords. Most importantly, traditional multiculturalists believe that equity means that funding Church of England, Roman Catholic and Jewish schools must also mean state funding for Muslim and Hindu schools where there is sufficient demand, as there often clearly is.

*After Multiculturalism,* we need to take a different approach – to fairly represent the society we live in without breaking it up further into minority groups aided and abetted by the State. The Church of England would be disestablished; the blasphemy laws should be scrapped, not extended, and there should not be state-funding for state schools of any religion. All schools can and should teach about the importance of faith to many instead of imposing secular liberal beliefs on all children. But religion itself should not be practised in any state-funded school. The citizenship education model wisely introduced by New Labour is an important new step. Within this framework, children are taught about universal human rights, civic responsibility, gender and race equality, mutual respect and the importance of questioning information and ideas.

## Education

*Traditional multiculturalism* takes what remains a highly Eurocentric curriculum, and bolts on Diwali, Martin Luther King and anti-racist policies. Home cultures of black and Asian children are revered and those of white children ignored. It is essentially an education of redress and cultural competition, not an education which teaches children the skills of critical interrogation. It is more interested in 'black' history than a history which connects and tells honest truths. It does not focus on the need to extend the appeal of Shakespeare to enable black and Asian children to feel this is part of their heritage and cannot see that white children need to see Benjamin Zefaniah as their poet too.

*After multiculturalism* we should take a very different view. Education must focus on providing children with the tools and skills they will need to thrive in a diverse society and interconnected world. Citizenship needs to teach all children the skills of critical interrogation, so that they are equipped to participate in and deal with the debates which our society needs to have. Instead of international citizenship education being about the United Nations and development education in a way which seems far-away and 'out there', these issues must be linked to the here and now and the international role and responsibilities which we need to play. New technologies can increasingly be used in exciting ways in schools to make these links real. All children need to learn about their own, shared and interconnected histories. In the early years of the Northern Ireland peace process, Irish and British historians worked together to interrogate the competing views of history which were taught in schools and to agree new texts which told the full and complex stories from all sides. We need to ensure that our best historians, like Linda Colley and Sunil Khilnani, who have rediscovered the complexities of our past, engage in similar projects with leading historians of former British colonies to help us to arrive at a better understanding of the many interactions which have ultimately shaped us all – and so that the opium wars, the potato famine or the Amritsar massacre are understood rather than providing the potential for festering sores to damage our international relationships many decades later. This should happen within the European Union too. It is striking how French textbooks talk about Austerlitz but not Waterloo, while British children are taught about world war one and the battle of Britain but not the foundation of the European Union.

## The Family

*Traditional multiculturalism* too often falsely perceives cultures to be self-contained and static. It encourages the conservatives within groups who want to 'preserve' and punish, and not permit the members of their communities to dissent or evolve. It simply fails to protect the human rights of many citizens who can be oppressed under the banner of laissez-faire multicultural diversity. Some women and children become victims and leave the communities or are destroyed by them.

In the end, the communities themselves are seriously damaged. When young girls are taken out of school in their teens and forced into marriages abroad, teachers, social work professionals and others feel they should steer clear in spite of being worried – they can be paralysed by being told that it is wrong to interfere.

And this kind of multiculturalism also fails to communicate the strengths of certain cultural practices across different communities. For example, divorce rates are very low in the Asian communities. Some of this is as a result of the dangerous containment of unhappiness but there is indisputable evidence of greater stability within these groups. The old multicultural way of thinking keeps this good news within the ghettoes. Adoption policies are still based on simplistic ethnic categories, leading to many failures. Today mixed-race children are seriously over-represented in the care system and few are willing to accept that old multiculturalism which labels all of them 'black' is partly responsible for which so few of them find homes or the kind of care they need within institutions. In one local authority in which I was researching, there had been a number of 'misplacements'. For example, a half-Iranian, half-Chinese child had been fostered by an African family – leading to a crisis and the child coming back into care. There were a number of such failures.

*After multiculturalism*, we need to rethink our approach to marriage, divorce and adoption. Diversity is to be encouraged but only if it does not violate basic universal principles. The rights of children and adults who are victimised by their own should take precedence over group cultural rights, through an inclusive debate involving, engaging and empowering all voices in our communities. The values of secular liberalism must be properly debated and may, at times, even be discarded as the cost paid by families in a culture overtaken by excessive individualism is questioned by all kinds of Britons. Mutual exchange should be encouraged and family institutions must always operate with this in mind. The roles of men and women should not be 'ethnicised' but dealt with in a broader framework so that the positive features in all British communities feed in to create a bedrock of values. The growing equality between white men and women is something many Asians aspire to. The valuing of older family members common in black and Asian families provides lessons for many white Britons.

Children in care would be set free from the old constraints of simple and easy identities. The central question should be 'what is the best thing our society can do in the interests of this child?'. When in children's homes, the trainers would be trained to treat the children as complex individuals and not as categories. Mixed-race children would be placed with suitable parents of all backgrounds as long as they understand racism and the importance of cultural identification.

## Crime, justice and human rights

Traditional multiculturalism sees law and order as a racial issue, rather than one about security and justice. While people have rightly been critical of the failures to tackle racism in the police force, the atmosphere of mutual mistrust between black and Asians and the police can create a damaging stand-off which does nothing to stop crime. Many people from across the community have suffered from a situation where white officers are still reluctant to go into certain largely black estates, while some black and Asian people are still uneasy about reporting crimes to the police. The real victims of no-go areas in our cities are the black, Asian and white people who live there. This situation is not helped by the fact that some liberal commentators still seem more concerned about the make-up of the police force than its effectiveness in dealing with crimes. These racially-defined responses to crime are replicated in multiculturalism's approach to rights. Traditional multiculturalism promotes the right of everybody to live within their own cultures, and this privileging of group and community rights extends to immunity from criticism from those outside the culture. It will protect the rights of different groups with their own campaigning bodies – for ethnic minorities, for women and for the disabled - which preach to the converted and argue with each other about who should have priority.

*After multiculturalism* we must persevere with the government's attempts to tackle – and be seen to tackle - racism, corruption and incompetence in the police force. The failures of the past mean that all police activities are seen through a negative prism by many black and Asian people. We must make the police force more representative – not to meet ethnic monitoring targets, but because it will become more effective at solving crime by winning the trust of the whole community. And because we are tackling institutional racism, we must not be afraid to condemn increases in crime whoever commits them, not to think that being from an 'ethnic minority' makes a criminal the victim. When dealing with different views of what rights mean, we need to realise that all cultures are diverse and changing, that they cannot fail to interact, and that they are all are subject to scrutiny and to mutually enriching dialogue in our national conversation and debates. The balance between equality and difference will have to be struck. There can be no sacrosanct cultures or spheres within them and no pressures to conform automatically to the dominant culture. To put this into practice, we should replace the Commission for Racial Equality and the Equal Opportunities Commission - with a Human Rights Commission taking responsibility for all of these areas of citizenship rights, opportunities and internationalism. Instead of being asserted separately as competing fringe minority issues, these interests should be reconciled and resolved. This sort of body would be better equipped to deal with differences within communities, not just between them. The Commission should draw upon the best practice of models abroad – including in Australia, Canada and New Zealand – and seek to play a prominent public role in ensuring that domestic debates about citizenship, rights and responsibilities are located in the broader global context.

## Arts and Media

*Traditional multiculturalism* counts the heads of different minority groups, creates special interest programming to cater for individual ethnic groups, and keeps diversity in these narrowly confined spaces while failing to alter the overall assumptions and output. Few black and Asian people are permitted to participate in the major debates of the nation and the world-view expressed is almost wholly white, often tied to Imperial fantasies. Much energy is put into counting how many 'ethnic minority' people work at the institutions and how they are represented. Much less attention is paid to how the assumptions, the ideals and creativity itself need to move into a broader more diverse, less comfortable world. Ethnic programmes are allowed to exist as long as they are safe. There was no programme on any of the ethnic slots which dealt with the damage caused by the narrow visions of Margaret Thatcher, for example.

*After multiculturalism,* we should think a lot harder about what is in the news, not just the colour of the people on our screens reading it. Our media institutions need to think much harder about how their output can best reflect a more globalised world and the role of this nation within it, just as the BBC has had to engage with and respond to the changes which devolution has brought to the United Kingdom. The question 'how many Brits' would not entirely dominate decisions on how and whether to cover international events. Now that many vital decisions are taken in multilateral fora, the importance of political change in other EU countries to Britain ought to be reflected in better coverage and explanations of elections and political change in Italy, Germany, France and the rest of the EU – to better balance exhaustive coverage of the New Hampshire primaries. The British broadsheet press has often said more about Joschka Fischer's suits than his policies. If we are to have national conversations about identity and ethics, it will be more important for key programmes such as *The Moral Maze, Question Time* and *Review* to present and interrogate a wide range of perspectives than to have George Alagiah presenting the news. This would require major shifts in mindset from what often seems, on Radio 4 for example, an endless diet of diplomatic wives, whites travelling abroad and how sad it is that Hong Kong had to be handed back. Rather than believing that we know exactly how the rest of the world sees us, we should do much more to examine and test these assumptions. One rare example of a new approach is *Dateline London* on the much-maligned News 24, where foreign and British journalists debate international affairs together. It should not be so extraordinary to hear dialogue involving views from Russia, the US, India, Africa or Arab countries on Blair, Kosovo, Zimbabwe or nuclear proliferation – especially when the views of politicians and publics abroad increasingly play a vital role in the success of our international policies. In the arts, there have been important shifts from The British Council and the Arts Council. They used to take an 'arts and crafts' approach to 'minority cultures', often training artists of particular races to rediscover their 'lost' cultural traditions. Increasingly they are most interested in the work of creative artists who are redefining identities, often by taking elements from different cultures and fusing them to create something entirely new. Artists like Asian Dub Foundation have done this and shown how it can appeal to mainstream audiences. It is vital that subsidised arts, theatre – and increasingly film

– production does not treat minority output as a separate question but ensures that 'mainstream' output is broadened, interrogating and challenging views of identity today. *East is East* is not a play or film about Asians – it is about the often painful process by which white and black people are forming something new, about the emergence of New Britain.

## Business and Employment

*Traditional multiculturalism* encourages businesses to promote ethnic monitoring, and to focus their recruitment policies so that all the equal opportunities rituals are followed. To fill in continuing gaps, targets are set and training courses are organised so that the 'ethnic minorities' can begin from a level playing field. But these approaches have had a very limited impact. The success stories which multiculturalism promotes are often of those who need little help – blacks and Asians who are well-educated and have the talent to get to the top. Because multiculturalism is seen as singling groups out as special and delivering favours, often to those who do not need them, there is opposition and resentment from those who feel that they are being adversely affected - yet there has not been a real breakthrough against discrimination. We know that Asian and black Britons are often over-represented on the more 'respected' university courses such as law, medicine and pharmacy yet they remain underrepresented at the top of professions. As Colin Brown observes: "Considering the years that have passed and the work that has been put in, the surprising fact is not that some people have hewn a niche in the business world or become professionally qualified but that so few have been allowed to succeed ... progress has been most evident where the acceptance, endorsement and help of white employers has been least required: in self-employment and the professions".[33] The major individual economic successes in black and Asian communities have rarely come out of equal opportunity and multicultural policies but from opting out. Parallel labour markets have been created, both in the successes of Asian business networks and the failures because too many people remain excluded.

*After multiculturalism*, we need to ensure that valuing diversity is seen as being about enabling everybody to succeed, not special treatment for favoured minorities. Only then will we tackle discrimination and inequalities more effectively. In practice, this would mean being much more robust about using existing legal remedies to tackle racism and exclusion – not just because it is good for black and Asian Britons but because equal opportunities must be central to the shared values of a fair society. And it will mean understanding racism within a broader context of exclusion and inequalities, so that we can deal with forms of exclusion which the multicultural agenda has not yet tackled. There is social exclusion at the bottom – starting with the asylum seekers who are qualified doctors and nurses but who work, illegally, as cleaners and taxi drivers. Even granted the right to work, asylum seekers, like other immigrants, face a range of barriers – from failures to recognise qualifications or make it easy to convert them, to the ability to deal successfully with the complexity of the system and inadequate knowledge among employers of what the rules are. We should have a skills audit for those asylum seekers who are here, to discover what skills they have and how they map to this country's needs. It will take state investment to upgrade skills and to provide language training required to use English for professional purposes, and broader reforms on issues like qualifications to tackle bureaucratic barriers to inclusion. But this could quite often be the quickest and least-expensive way to deal with the gaps which are crippling some surgeries and hospitals. There is also exclusion of those who are relatively well-off. We need to find out more about why many well-qualified blacks and Asians are not entering the mainstream economy, and also to find ways to tap the knowledge which is contained within family and community businesses. Within companies, diversity programmes need to based not around increasing the numbers of blacks and Asians and then introducing schemes to deal with the diversity which they are said to bring to the workforce, but on a very clear message that many forms of diversity are central to modern life – and that dealing successfully with this, with employees, suppliers and customers at home and abroad is essential for enlightened self-interest. Some companies are now taking this on board – it is the linguistic diversity of the south-east of England that attracts investment from call centres to banks. Only when we recognise that diversity is now one of the central assets of Great Britain PLC – but that it is much broader than is usually recognised – can we transform this debate into a productive one. As James Lynch of the World Bank has said "the overlapping dimensions of Britain's diversity, across a large number of  overlapping cultural factors and dimensions, represents a pluralism of pluralisms which are not usually embraced within the academic and political discourse about diversity in this society".

## Immigration, Trade and Industry

*Traditional multiculturalism* has naturally been critical of many of the assumptions and practices of British immigration policy. But many black and Asian Britons, thinking narrowly in multicultural ways, are hostile to asylum seekers applying to enter Britain. In part it is because they have taken on the xenophobic values of many small islanders; in part it is because they fear that more 'minorities' means less for them in this already begrudging place.

*After multiculturalism* we need a more rational approach. Immigration must be decoupled from race relations with a new approach based not on race but on economic need and international human rights obligations. Demographers show how Europe, with its ageing societies and low birth rates, will require the energy of more immigrants to sustain economic success. *The Economist* has consistently argued for more liberal and rational immigration policies. So it will be important to release the British population from their own panic about hordes of immigrants – our good life may depend on it. This will be politically difficult in a society where immigration has been seen as something to control, a threat and not an asset. But the process of change, begun with early changes in the immigration rules and the Home Office's decision to stop using the term 'bogus', must be maintained and based on a clear intellectual case to avoid mixed messages being sent out.

Immigration policies should be based on clearly set-out criteria, which are not detached from the policies of the DTI, the Foreign Office, and the needs of the country, but which respond to these. In Canada, this sort of points system has meant that the country has maximised the benefits which it gains from immigration. In Silicon Valley, computer experts from certain Indian universities are vied for by American firms because their skills are valued. These experts make their money and then often return to India to develop the industry in their homeland. In order to work, Britain needs to be defined as the country of immigration and emigration which it has been forever. We need to recognise the benefits which have accrued from this – the fact that Asian and Chinese millionaires here mean real penetration into these markets and businesses; that all day shopping and the heart transplant supremo Magdi Yacoub are both the result of immigration. We Ugandan Asians reluctantly accepted in 1972 have created 30,000 jobs in the Midlands. German economists have provided a cost-benefit analysis of migrant labour, concluding that taxpayers would have had to pay much higher taxes had there not been migrant workers. Attitudes can be changed as alternative narratives begin to saturate public consciousness. Canada marks out national days to celebrate immigrants through the centuries, involving all groups and peoples. True globalisation should mean the freer movement of skills and people as well as capital and jobs. With more open immigration policies illegal immigration would decline and fewer people would be criminalised for doing exactly what white Britons have done for centuries – seeking their fortunes in Australia, Canada and now South Africa. And since it is business that will need the skills that immigrants can bring, so that we don't lose out to Silicon Valley or Bangalore in the skills race that is driving the knowledge economy, business should campaign as strongly to policy-makers and the public on this as they do on corporation tax.

On asylum policy, to fulfil their obligations under international human rights treaties and conventions, the British government should also make clear commitments – every three years – on the maximum number of asylum seekers who will be admitted and state clearly that the size of the country means that it is impossible to absorb more, unless there is a major catastrophe requiring renegotiation. More information needs to be provided on the causes of refugee flows and on how asylum seekers are settling down, re-migrating or returning by tracking them better. We need to be clear that it is not possible to take in all the asylum seekers who wish to come here – but an internationalist sensibility would ensure that we are all much better informed about where the trouble spots are around the world and would want to do more to tackle the root causes of refugee flows. It would be sceptical of politicians who tried to foster prejudice against asylum seekers and would seek instead to be told the facts; that there are genuine refugees who cannot all be given asylum because of demographic pressures on this small island, but that we have a duty to play our part.

## Foreign Policy

*Traditional multiculturalism* has never been very interested in foreign policy or international issues, except perhaps on narrow, group-based lobbying issues. And this is why foreign policy and international relations discourse has tended to see diaspora influence as likely to distract and disrupt, to be a threat and a danger. Traditional multiculturalism is also often represented at its worst in the tokenistic and useless initiatives of some international institutions which want to say that they are 'doing their bit', but where almost nobody knows or hears much at all about what these initiatives actually do. The European Union has traditionally been amongst the worst offenders, with tokenistic representations of minority groups tacked-on to a very western, Christian and partial conception of Europe's history. Multiculturalism can also lead to our feeling inhibited when it comes to clear-cut examples where human rights are being violated, for fear of being accused of cultural imperialism, even when groups on the ground are calling for international engagement. Regimes which abuse rights have become adept at exploiting multicultural language to cover up their own failings, while many western commentators of both left and right collude in this.

*After multiculturalism,* we need to ensure that we can use all of this country's resources in a way that will maximise British interests and our contribution to a stable and fair international order. We need to understand that this country can play a pivotal role in facilitating internationalism not just through its membership of global multilateral institutions but through the make-up of our society. If Britain can be clear that we have left behind our imperial past and mindset then we can be robust in promoting and protecting the democratic values which all Britons and people across the world in our emerging international society share today.

In the debate about international intervention, Britain should continue the push to create rules which can be consistently applied, based on the seriousness of the threat to human rights and to international order and the ability of the international community to make an effective difference. Britain should continue to be clear that our responses will not be based on the ethnicity of those involved – so that we react to a crisis in Sierra Leone as well as in Zimbabwe, and that we understand the Zimbabwe crisis as a question of political repression affecting blacks as well as white farmers. Nor should geographical boundaries provide a limit to our response, so that there would next time be concerted international effort in a case like that of Rwanda as well as Kosovo. Of course, this does not mean that there will be an identical response in every case or that we will be always best placed to intervene. The realities of what is possible in dealing with human rights abuses in Chechnya or Tibet determine how far outsiders can effectively intervene. And the best solutions will often be regional solutions – not just because these are less likely to be rejected as 'western imperialism' but because local actors will often have greater local knowledge and credibility. But the broader international community does need to be engaged and to do more to build regional and local capabilities to respond effectively to crises.

When Britain is directly involved, our contribution will be

effective when it responds to local need and is credible with the people who we are trying to work with. British embassies already employ increasing numbers of locally-engaged staff on the ground – but there should no longer be a glass-ceiling on how high these people can rise. We should also ensure that we have desk-level expertise in London which draws on the deep links which this country has with Nigeria, India and many other places around the world. It needs to be understood that increases in locally-engaged staff and the number of black and Asian Britons being employed in our diplomatic service are not being pursued for tokenistic reasons of image, or even simply to be fair to these groups, but because effective solutions often need the particular in-depth knowledge and expertise which these people can bring in – either in situations of foreign policy crises, as in Yemen, or in terms of the deep links which British Iranians have with the democratic, reformist and feminist movements in Iran.

For all Britons to be much more involved in the debate about the European Union and other international issues, we need to link Britain's goals to domestic debates and values, so that the national interest is understood concretely in terms of jobs, crime and the environment, and how quality-of-life for all can be improved. The European Union can be seen as almost a classically 'multicultural' political system, with the fifteen nations being the groups represented – with a French, British or Italian position on every issue, and jobs shared out by nationality rather than merit. We need to reshape these debates so that they are based on transferring best practice around the EU, and so that they allow political parties, citizens and the media to debate the values behind policies and not just their national origins. To work, this will need to be underpinned by a vision of Europe which is broad and exciting enough to include everybody – which isn't just based on fifteen imagined blood nations but makes an asset of the contributions of British Pakistanis or guestworkers in Germany, and which lives up to the values and rights that Europe proclaims by delivering for them too.

The Commonwealth provides one example of how institutions can develop the potential to evolve in a post-multicultural direction. Given its imperial roots, it is not surprising that it went through a classically multicultural period, able to act cohesively on little beyond apartheid. But it now has an ability to be based on new forms of global links based on new common purposes in the future, whether strengthening democratisation or creating a fairer and more open global system. While the Commonwealth Institute used to have an alcove for every country in its displays, it is now involved in e-Commonwealth networking and sharing of best practice.

Across the field of foreign policy, Britain's contribution and ability to deliver is strengthened when we can link our involvement not just to our global history but to the values and identity of Britain today. Britain does have a unique role at the centre of many of the world's international institutions – the UN, the EU, the G8 and the Commonwealth – but, even more important to our role as a potential 'global joiner' are the 'living links' of Britain's diasporas and broader society with communities around the world. We need to facilitate and invest in these links more, because they deliver important benefits to Britain internationally. They help to tackle out-of-date perceptions that Britain has not changed in its make-up or international approach; these can persist because perceptions abroad will always take some time to match domestic developments, because we in Britain sometimes remain ambivalent about our global histories and future, or because it suits the political purposes of others to argue that Britain remains stuck in the imperial or insular past.

*After multiculturalism* there will be new challenges for all of us if we are to participate fully in a new debate about who we are and what we can achieve together. If the multiculturalism debate has not delivered what many of us had hoped it might it has, for all of its incompleteness and inconsistencies, provided the platform from which we must build a new, more inclusive and outward-looking approach. The scale of the challenges both at home and abroad should not be underestimated – there will need to be continuing struggles to eliminate racism, fear, the many forms of inequality and inclusion which there are today. But, in fighting these battles, we must always be inspired by a vision – and it must be one in which our dreams are not limited or constrained either by fixed assumptions or national boundaries. There may be important differences between us – but they can and must be bridged. However hard a few may try, our society can not now be broken down into monolithic ethnic tribes. We need to understand that, by turning outwards together, we can make our diversity a source of strength for the new Britain we are trying to create, rather than a new set of dividing lines which hold us back.

# Endnotes

1   *The Economist*, 6th November 1999

2   Stuart Hall interviewed by Yasmin Alibhai-Brown for *National Portrait,*
    Analysis, BBC Radio 4, 2nd December 1999

3   Yasmin Alibhai-Brown, *'Islam and the Euro-Identity'* Demos Collection 13,
    1998

4   In the draft report of the Commission on the Future of Multiethnic Britain
    due out in September 2000

5   See Yasmin Alibhai-Brown, *'Who Do We Think We Are?'* (Penguin, 2000)
    Chapter two

6   Mike and Trevor Phillips, *Windrush* (Harper Collins, 1998)

7   Ali Rattansi, 'Changing the Subject? Racism, Culture and Education', in
    James Donald and Ali Rattansi (ed): *'Race', Culture and Difference* (Open
    University/Sage, 1992), p15

8   Interviews carried out by the author, January 2000

9   See Yasmin Alibhai-Brown and Anne Montague, *The Colour of Love*
    (Virago Press 1991)

10  Paul Goodman interviewed by Yasmin Alibhai-Brown for *National Portrait,*
    Analysis, op cit.

11  Bhikhu Parekh, quoted by Stuart Hall in *The Multicultural Question*

12  See Abul Taher, 'Call to Arms', *Education, The Guardian*, 16th May 2000

13  An interview in *Connections, Winter 1999/2000*

14  Andrew Marr, *The Day Britain Died*, BBC2, 2nd February 2000

15  See for example Sivanandan`s searing essay 'RAT and the Degradation of
    Black Struggles', *Race and Class* Vol.25, no.4, Institute of Race Relations,
    1985

16  Narinder Minhas, 'Look on the white side', *The Guardian*, 10th January
    2000

17  *European Youth Survey, MTV, February 1997*

18  Roger Hewitt, *Routes of Racism, The Social Basis of Racist Action*
    (Trentham Books)

19  See Yasmin Alibhai-Brown, *'Who Do We Think We Are?'* (Penguin, 2000)
    Chapter one

20  Andrew Marr, *The Day Britain Died* (Profile Books, 2000) p146

21  *Linda Colley, Britishness in the 21st Century,* Downing Street Millennium
    Lectures, 8th December 1999. See www.number-10.gov.uk for full text

22  Marr, op.cit, p134

23  Ron Takaki, *A Different Mirror* (Little, Brown 1993), p17

24  Takaki, op. cit. p429

25  Maya Jaggi, 'Casting off the shackles of history', *The Guardian*, 3rd November 1999

26  Yasmin Alibhai-Brown, 'Sacred Beauty', *Guardian Weekend*, 15th January 2000

27  Caryl Phillips (ed) *Extravagant Strangers: a Literature of belonging* (Faber and Faber 1997)

28  Stuart Hall, *Unsettling 'The Heritage': Re-imagining the post-nation*, Conference speech for 'Whose Heritage?' Published by the Arts Council, 1999, p15

29  Stuart Hall interview with Yasmin Alibhai-Brown for National Portrait, Analysis, op. cit.

30  See Pico Iyer, '*The Nowhere Man*' in *Prospect* February 1997 and more recently '*Stranger in a Strange Land*', *Prospect* February 2000

31  She made these arguments forcefully on 'Start The Week', BBC Radio 4, February 21st, 2000

32  Personal communication, 18th January, 2000

33  Colin Brown, 'Racial Disadvantage in the Employment Market' in Brahm et al (ed) *Racism and Anti-Racism* (Open University Press, 1992), p63

# Also available from The Foreign Policy Centre

Individual publications should be ordered from Central Books,
99 Wallis Road, London, E9 5LN tel: 020 8986 5488, fax: 020 8533 5821
email: mo@centralbooks.com

## THE FOREIGN POLICY CENTRE MISSION STATEMENT
March 1999; Free, with £1 p+p, or free with any pamphlet
*'Likely to be controversial with Mandarins and influential with Ministers'*
*Financial Times*


## GOING PUBLIC: DIPLOMACY FOR THE INFORMATION SOCIETY
Mark Leonard and Vidhya Alakeson, The Foreign Policy Centre
May 2000; £9.95 plus £1 p+p. ISBN 0-9535598-7-4
In an age of global communications, building links with overseas publics
will matter as much to foreign policy as talking to governments. Whether
Britain wants a lasting coalition for international action in Kosovo, the
French to lift the beef ban or Russia to become a stable democracy, influ-
encing people abroad must be central to our strategy. The usual diplomatic
channels can't do this on their own. The Foreign Office must unleash the
energy of 60 million budding ambassadors in Britain's schools, businesses,
local authorities, political parties and communities to build deeper links
across the world. Going Public shows how Britain should fuse the strengths
of traditional and public diplomacy to build the relationships we need to
thrive in a globalised world.
*The project is supported by the BBC World Service, The British Council, and the
Design Council.*


## RE-ENGAGING RUSSIA
John Lloyd, journalist and member of The Foreign Policy Centre's advisory council
March 2000; £9.95, plus £1 p+p. ISBN 0-9535598-6-6
*Published in association with BP Amoco*
*'Re-engaging Russia is excellent on where Russia's relationships with the west
went wrong ... thought-provoking, highly-enjoyable, creative and timely'*
*Keith Vaz, Minister for Europe*

*'Characteristically thoughtful and well-written, the pamphlet by this outstand-
ing journalist and Russia-watcher recognises the failures both of post-Soviet
Russia and of western policy towards that country. John Lloyd argues convinc-
ingly that the answer is not for the west to disengage in Russia but to engage
differently'*
*Professor Archie Brown, St Antony's College Oxford*

## GLOBALIZATION – KEY CONCEPTS, Number One

David Held & Anthony McGrew, David Goldblatt & Jonathan Perraton
April 1999; £4.95, plus £1 p+p. ISBN 0-9535598-0-7

Globalization is the buzz-word of the age – but how many people understand it? In this much-needed concise and authoritative guide, globalization's leading theorists thrash out what it really means, and argue that we need to rethink politics to keep up with the changing shape of power.

*'An indispensable counterweight to optimists and pessimists alike'*
**Will Hutton, The Observer**


## NETWORK EUROPE

Mark Leonard, The Foreign Policy Centre
September 1999; £9.95, plus £1 p+p. ISBN 0-9535598-2-3
*Published in association with Clifford Chance*

A radical new agenda for European reform, arguing that pro-Europeans must reshape the European debate if Europe is to be both effective and popular. Instead of the traditional federalist reform agenda, the EU should learn from successful network models of business organisation and introduce elements of direct democracy to reconnect to its citizens.

*'A welcome contribution to the important debate about Europe's future'*
**Rt Hon Tony Blair MP, Prime Minister**

*'A radical agenda for reform from the government's favourite foreign policy think-tank'*
**Stephen Castle, Independent on Sunday**


## NEW VISIONS FOR EUROPE:
## The Millennium Pledge

Mark Leonard, Vidhya Alakeson and Stephen Edwards, The Foreign Policy Centre
November 1999; £2.95, plus £1 p+p ISBN 0-9535598-5-8
*Published in association with Clifford Chance*

A proposed commitment from the governments to the peoples of Europe, outlining the approach and policy reforms which could help to reconnect the EU to its citizens

## REINVENTING THE COMMONWEALTH

Kate Ford and Sunder Katwala, The Foreign Policy Centre

November 1999; £9.95, plus £1 p+p. ISBN 0-9535598-1-5

*Published in association with the Royal Commonwealth Society*

Launched at the Durban Heads of Government Meeting, this report shows how wide-ranging Commonwealth reform could create a modern, effective and relevant organisation – helping members to thrive in the 21st century by creating an internationally-recognised standard for good governance and the conditions for investment.

*'Wide-reaching and intelligent'* **The Times**

## MAKING THE COMMONWEALTH MATTER – Interim Report

Kate Ford and Sunder Katwala, The Foreign Policy Centre

April 1999; £4.95, plus £1 p+p. ISBN 0-9535598-1-5

*'The biggest shake-up of the Commonwealth since it was set up in its present form 50 years ago'* **The Independent on Sunday**

## TRADING IDENTITIES: Why countries and companies are taking on each others' roles

Wally Olins, co-founder of Wolff Olins, branding and identity consultant.

October 1999; £9.95, plus £1 p+p ISBN 0-9535598-3-1

Countries and companies are changing fast – and they are becoming more like each other. As countries develop their 'national brands' to compete for investment, trade and tourism, mega-merged global companies are using nation-building techniques to achieve internal cohesion across cultures and are becoming ever more involved in providing public services like education and health. Wally Olins asks what these cross-cutting trends mean for the new balance of global power.

*'a fascinating pamphlet'*, **Peter Preston, The Guardian**

# Forthcoming publications

## EUROPE: WINNING THE ARGUMENT
Robert M Worcester, Chairman, MORI International

Can pro-Europeans convince the public on Europe? 25 years after the 1975 referendum, Bob Worcester looks at the lessons for the Europe debate now – looking at how referendums are won, how public opinion is formed and how it can be shifted and which arguments are likely to prove decisive in a referendum on the Euro in the future.

## DEMOCRATISING GLOBAL GOVERNANCE (prov)
### Rights and Responsibilities of NGOs
Michael Edwards, Director of Governance, Ford Foundation

Is the rise of NGOs an important democratising force or a damaging threat to political debate and representation. NGOs have spread participation, forged north-south links and spoken up for human rights. But they face increasing scrutiny as questions are asked – often by developing country governments – about the legitimacy, accountability and integrity of NGOs themselves. Who do they represent and how? Are they a force for global participation or a new form of western imperialism? Michael Edwards seeks to avoid a damaging stand-off between NGOs, governments and international organisations by finding new ways to reconstruct global cooperation.

## THE POST-MODERN STATE AND THE NEW WORLD ORDER
Robert Cooper, Cabinet Office (writing in a personal capacity)
2nd edition. Published in association with Demos.

What did 1989 really mean? Robert Cooper argues that the end of the Cold War also marked the end of the balance-of-power system in Europe. Yet today's open, multilateral post-modern states must deal with a complex world – where many states follow traditional realpolitik, while collapsed and failing states present the dangers of pre-modern chaos. The second edition of this groundbreaking pamphlet also addresses how the role of religion in international politics is very different today.

## RETHINKING SOVEREIGNTY (prov)

David Held, Professor of Politics and Sociology, Open University

What does sovereignty mean today, when the collective fortunes of peoples are increasingly intertwined? David Held examines how changes in security, economics, communications and political activism are reshaping ideas of political community. How should democracy and politics keep up with the changing shape of power?

## MODERNISING ISLAM

Ziauddin Sardar, writer and broadcaster

This timely, controversial and challenging report argues that the Muslim diaspora, far from being a threat and mere agents of a global Islamic fundamentalist agenda, can play a positive role in updating Islam.

## DEMOCRATISING GLOBAL SPORT

Sunder Katwala, The Foreign Policy Centre

Sporting scandals have shaken many major sports to their foundations. This report will address how the governance of international sport can cope with an age of globalisation, commercialisation and accountability – proposing reforms to better reconcile the interests of athletes, supporters, sponsors, broadcasters, officials and the game as a whole in the spirit of fair play.

## THE KIDNAPPING BUSINESS

Rachel Briggs, The Foreign Policy Centre

The nature of kidnapping is changing: an important political tool is now a sophisticated business and the gap left by policy makers has been filled by kidnap and ransom insurance. This project will assess these new trends and work towards a new integrated policy response. This project is supported by Hiscox, Control Risks Group, SCR, J&H Marsh and McLennan and ASM.

## THE HIDDEN WEALTH OF NATIONS

Hernando de Soto, President, Institute for Liberty and Democracy, Lima

Can capitalism work in the developing world? Hernando de Soto – described by Time magazine as one of the five leading Latin American "Leaders for the next millennium" and author of *The Other Path* – provides an entirely new model for a successful transition to the market, which can empower the 5 billion people left out of global prosperity to date. Policymakers need to recognise that the poor have already, against the odds, accumulated the assets needed to succeed at capitalism – but because they operate in the illegal economy, their 'dead capital' can not be put to productive use. Drawing on experience at the heart of policy-making in Latin America, Asia and Africa, de Soto provides a road-map which can transform the debate about development.

# Subscribe to The Foreign Policy Centre

The Foreign Policy Centre offers a number of ways for people to get involved. Our subscription scheme keeps you up-to-date with our work, with at least six free publications each year and our quarterly newsletter, Global Thinking. Subscribers also receive major discounts on events and further publications.

## Subscriptions

| TYPE OF SUBSCRIPTION | PRICE |
| --- | --- |
| ● Individuals | £50 |
| ● Concessions (students, OAPs, JSA) | £25 |
| ● Organisations | £150 |
| ● Libraries (will receive ALL publications) | £200 |

Please make cheques payable to The Foreign Policy Centre, indicating clearly your postal and email address and the appropriate package and send to The Foreign Policy Centre, Panton House, 25 Haymarket, London SW1Y 4EN.

## The Foreign Policy Centre Diplomatic Partnership

The Foreign Policy Centre Diplomatic Partnership is aimed at the key
embassy players. It is an ideal way for embassies to keep up to date with
the work of The Foreign Policy Centre and will provide a useful
environment for ideas sharing.

Members will receive the following benefits:

- Special invitations to attend The Foreign Policy Centres annual
  Diplomatic Forum, which will be led by a high-profile speaker, bringing
  together key embassy players to address one or more of the foreign
  policy issues of the day
- Three free copies of every The Foreign Policy Centre publication
- Three free copies of *Global Thinking*, The Foreign Policy Centre's
  newsletter
- VIP invitations for up to three embassy representatives to all Foreign
  Policy Centre public events

Membership of The Foreign Policy Centre Diplomatic Partnership is £500
per year.

## The Foreign Policy Centre Business Partnership

The Foreign Policy Centre also runs a Business Partnership scheme, which
aims to bring the business community to the heart of foreign policy thinking.

For more details about this scheme, please contact Rachel Briggs, Corporate
Affairs Manager - rachel@fpc.org.uk

# AFTER MULICULTURALISM

Yasmin Alibhai-Brown

Yasmin Alibhai-Brown argues that we need to fundamentally rethink our approach to national identity, race and public culture. The old debate about multiculturalism cannot meet the challenge of reinventing identity and participation in a devolved Britain, a plural Europe and an increasingly inter-dependent world. We need to leave behind a debate which has too often only engaged blacks, Asians and 'ethnic minorities' rather than whites as well. Yasmin shows how these discourses belong to a historical era which is now ending. She shows how we must create new ways of talking about who we are, and what this will mean in specific policy areas, if the coming battles over political culture and national identity are to have a progressive outcome.

**Yasmin Alibhai-Brown** is Senior Researcher at The Foreign Policy Centre. She has a weekly column in *The Independent*, and also writes for *The* Guardian, *The Observer* and many other newspapers. Yasmin also broadcasts regularly on Radio 4 and the World Service. Her most recent book is *Who Do We Think We Are? Imagining the New Britain*. Her previous books include *The Colour of Love, True Colours* and her autobiography *No Place Like Home*.

0953559882

£9.95
ISBN 0-9535598-8-2
Politics / Current Affa
Sociology / Globalisa
www.fpc.org.uk

**The Foreign Policy Centre**